The Lockheed Constellation

Above: *The Super Constellation prototype with, in the background, TWA Model L-749A N6014C Star of Delaware as yet unpainted*

Opposite: *Constellations on the ramp at Burbank shortly after VJ Day, with one of Eastern's in the foreground*

The Lockheed Constellation

by M. J. Hardy

ARCO PUBLISHING COMPANY, INC
New York

Published by Arco Publishing Company, Inc.
219 Park Avenue South, New York, N.Y. 10003

Copyright © 1973 by M. J. Hardy

Library of Congress Catalog Card Number 72-90332

ISBN 0 668 02885 8

Printed in Great Britain

Contents

Introduction

Selected as the subject for this first volume in a new series of David & Charles Aircraft Family Monographs, the Lockheed Constellation airliner, true to the Lockheed tradition for sleekness of line, has upheld the maxim that what looks good is good. When it first went into airline service in 1946 the Constellation surpassed every other transport aircraft in almost every aspect of performance and introduced such advanced features as pressurisation, hydraulic power-boosted controls, reversible-pitch airscrews and high-lift Fowler flaps. And as the type was developed by successive increases in weight, power, fuel capacity and payload, it came to achieve a unique 'triple crown' among post-war piston-engined airliners—operation of the first non-stop North Atlantic and US transcontinental services and of the first round-the-world service (by Qantas of Australia).

Although always primarily intended for international and domestic trunk routes, when it was finally displaced as first-line equipment by the jets in the 1960s, it demonstrated its qualities in the hands of a number of smaller airlines, charter and supplemental carriers in areas far off the beaten track and in operations of sometimes dubious legality. These included flying in support of oil-drilling operations in Northern Alaska, flying arms into the Yemen and Biafra, a number of smuggling ventures to South American countries, such as Bolivia and Paraguay, and even, in the role of makeshift bomber, an attack on the presidential palace of the Haitian dictator, the late 'Papa Doc' Duvalier. In particular, the Biafra airlift, largely maintained by Super Constellations, was a remarkable performance in terms of reliability considering the military and operational hazards involved and the lack of any major maintenance and overhaul facilities in the area.

The Connie was among the very first transports to test a collision-warning radar and weather radar, and its outstanding design qualities were well demonstrated during the vital part it played in the defence of the North American continent in the role of airborne early warning and radar picket. Big excrescences like the dorsal and ventral radomes, and the earlier Speedpak freight container, had surprisingly little effect on its handling characteristics and early warning/special electronics versions (some still classified) have continued to be developed, while some interesting one-off modifications of early warning aircraft for such jobs as oceanographic research and radiation measurement have been made. Few aircraft can have flown well with quite so many radome configurations as the Super Connie, these ranging from the WV-2E's saucer-shaped dorsal radome and no ventral radome to the ventral radome only of some one-off research aircraft. Different engines have likewise presented no difficulty and the prototype, 'Old 1961', flew powered at one and the same time by conventional piston engines, a Turbo-Compound and an Allison turboprop.

Although stressed from the outset for eventual conversion to turboprop power and flown extensively as a test-bed for such powerplants, the Super Constellation was fated never to go into production with engines of this category, and in the final production model with the new thinner 150ft-span wing the airframe development potential ran ahead of its Turbo-Compound engines. Had the big jets not dominated the scene in the 1960s and had Lockheed's design efforts not been engaged with the Electra and C-130 Hercules turboprops, the basic Model 1649A airframe would doubtless have been developed into turboprop versions and, as such, would undoubtedly have given the long-haul Bristol Britannia turboprop a run for its money. An outstanding example of piston-engined airliner design at its peak, the Constellation well befits the dictionary definition of its name as 'a group of fixed stars, or an assemblage of splendours or excellences'.

M. J. HARDY

Angmering, Sussex

1: Design Origins

It would be difficult to exaggerate the debt which modern airliner development owes to two factors in particular: the United States' belief in the benefits of airline competition (and a political and regulatory climate which has always seen to it that such benefits accrue to the travelling public) and, more particularly, the competitive requirements of the US transcontinental routes from New York through Chicago to Los Angeles or San Francisco. From the early 1930s onward, the three major US transcontinental airlines and their predecessor companies had been engaged in an increasingly stiff battle for transcontinental traffic, not only between themselves but also with the railroads, and the goal which each airline sought, of reducing its coast-to-coast time over that of its competitors and cutting the number of stops, led United Airlines, American Airlines and Transcontinental and Western Airlines (later Trans World Airlines) to sponsor not just one but a whole series of highly successful transport aircraft from the drawing-boards of Boeing, Douglas and Lockheed.

Too often there is a tendency outside the USA to think of America's dominance in airliner manufacture and sales as being due solely to the size of the home markets its industry enjoys; less obvious advantages are the pace of re-equipment and technological advance which a highly competitive environment makes possible—even before the war this was of very real benefit—and, to use the industry's jargon, the plurality of native user demand resulting from the number of competing airlines, and the broader specification writing that goes with it. Whether a type is sponsored by an individual airline, as the Lockheed Constellation was by TWA, or collectively by several carriers like its contemporary the Douglas DC-4, the value to US manufacturers of the feedback of operating experience and ideas for improvement from a number of vigorously competing user airlines has been, and is, immense, whether in developing stretched versions of the existing airframe or writing the specification for its successor, as well as in the more everyday business

of defect rectification and the introduction of minor modifications.

Starting with the Vega of 1927, Lockheed had produced a line of single-engined, small-capacity transports of exceptionally clean aerodynamic design for the period. The high-wing Vega was followed by the parasol-wing Air Express designed for Western Air Express, the low-wing Sirius mailplane, the two-seater Altair and the seven-seater Orion of 1932, the latter being the first production transport aircraft to have a retractable undercarriage. As well as by operators in the States, Orions were used by Swissair, and an increasing number of other European airlines were to follow this lead and buy from Douglas and Lockheed up to the outbreak of World War II. The Orion was followed in 1934 by the ten-passenger Model 10 Electra, the first of a line of twin-engined transports built to the modern formula of all-metal construction with retractable undercarriages, flaps and variable-pitch airscrews. The six-passenger Lockheed 12, of which 114 were built, followed in 1936 and the eleven-passenger Model 14 Super Electra in 1937, the latter being the first aircraft in airline service to feature fully-feathering airscrews, as well as underfloor freight holds and two-speed superchargers. A total of 112 Model 14s was built, as well as a hastily-designed maritime reconnaissance version, known as the Hudson, which was the first US type to be ordered in quantity by the Royal Air Force and saw widespread war service with Coastal Command and other Allied air forces. The Model 18 Lodestar, of which 625 in all were built, was a development of the Model 14 seating three more passengers. The Lockheed twins were complementary to, rather than competitive with, the larger 21-passenger DC-3, and sold to many smaller operators all over the world, as well as to larger airlines for their multi-stop feeder-type routes.

Yet the DC-3, highly successful though it was to be on coast-to-coast services, was not a long-haul aeroplane and in mid-1935, several months before it first flew, discussions started between Douglas, the 'Big

Four' domestic airlines and Pan American Airways about a new four-engined airliner for the trunk routes. The following March each of these airlines put up $100,000 (equivalent to £20,000 at that time) towards the design and construction of a prototype and this, the DC-4E, first flew on 7 June 1938. The DC-4E was evaluated by United Airlines over its routes in 1939 and received Civil Aeronautics Administration (CAA) certification on 5 May 1939. But in the end it did not go into production, as the five sponsor airlines felt that it was somewhat too large and incorporated too many advanced technical features which would require extensive development before being put into service. The type was then redesigned into the production DC-4, being scaled down a bit in the process and, in spite of its designation, became virtually a new aeroplane. Another contender began to take shape in mid-1936, while the DC-4E was still in the design stage, when Pan American Airways and TWA started discussions about a possible airliner development of the B-17 Flying Fortress high-altitude bomber, which had

first flown in the previous year. The result was the Boeing Model 307 Stratoliner, which used the same wings, tail unit and undercarriage of the B-17 married to a large-diameter circular-section fuselage designed for pressurisation. This feature had encouraged TWA to order six 307s and Pan American three in the spring of 1937, some time before the prototype first flew on 31 December 1938, Pan Am having helped to finance development of the pressure cabin.

The Excalibur Project

While the DC-4E was being evaluated, Lockheed joined Boeing in the long-haul airliner stakes with the L-44 Excalibur project, revealed in April 1939, which was to be the forerunner of the Constellation. This started as a 21-passenger aeroplane with a gross weight of 27,550lb and a single fin and rudder, and later grew to seat 26–30 passengers and to have the characteristic

The Excalibur project in its early form very much resembled a scaled-up, four-engined Model 10A Electra

In its final form the Excalibur had triple fins and rudders and seating for thirty-six passengers

Lockheed twin fins and rudders. Pan American showed some interest in the Excalibur but wanted more speed and capacity, and under their influence it grew into its final form as a 36-passenger aeroplane with triple fins and rudders and a deeper fuselage, similar in shape to the Lodestar's. It was now slightly smaller than the Boeing 307, with a wing of 95ft span and 1,000sq ft area, a nosewheel undercarriage, triple fins and rudders with fabric-covered control surfaces and the same engines as the 307—four 1,000hp Wright Cyclone GR-1820-G205A radials driving Hamilton Standard Hydromatic airscrews. Up to thirty-six passengers could be seated in a pressurised cabin not very much larger than that of the DC-3—30ft long, 7ft high and 9ft 2in wide—while baggage and freight compartments totalled 400cu ft in volume. The two-spar wing had improved Lockheed high-lift flaps, and it was intended to use a retractable shock-absorbing tail bumper for emergency use in such cases as the nose being raised too high for take-off. The nosewheel was steerable and there were brakes on all three wheels.

The fuel tankage was 1,200 US gal or 500 US gal less than the 307, while the loaded weight at 40,000lb was 5,000lb less than that of the Boeing design, having grown somewhat from its original 27,550–36,000lb. The estimated performance was appreciably faster

than the 307's, a maximum speed of 294mph at 15,300ft and a cruising speed of 247mph at 12,000ft being claimed, although the Excalibur would have had a shorter range. A projected 40-passenger version was studied under the designation L-144 but, in the end, the Excalibur did not get beyond the project stage, despite a provisional order for two placed by South African Airways when it ordered twenty-nine Lodestars for domestic and regional routes in April 1940. SAA had previously ordered two Junkers Ju 90 four-engined airliners to supplement its largely Junkers-equipped fleet of Ju 52/3ms and Ju 86s, but the outbreak of war prevented the Ju 90s from being delivered, and SAA did not operate Constellations until 1950.

The Constellation is Born

In April 1939, shortly before the Douglas contender in its original DC-4E form was dropped and a few months after the Boeing 307's maiden flight, Lockheed had started preliminary design work to a specification issued by TWA for an airliner capable of flying the transcontinental routes non-stop carrying a payload of 6,000lb for a still air range of 3,500 miles at between 250 and 300mph at 20,000ft. This project was the L-49, later designated L-049 and named 'Constellation', and was an enlarged development of the Excalibur approximating closely to the production DC-4 in size but with more power in the shape of four of the new Wright Duplex Cyclone R-3350-35 18-

cylinder two-row radials of 2,200hp each. This delivered 22 per cent more power than the next biggest Wright engine, the R-2600 Cyclone, but did so at a specific fuel consumption 26 per cent less—a remarkable achievement that was the key to the Constellation's success. This was the largest project Lockheed had yet embarked on and it is interesting, and not a little ironic in view of later events, to recall that the British and French purchasing missions that visited the United States in 1938 to place large orders found the US aircraft industry at a low ebb financially, and generally in a state of depression similar to that of the British industry before the rearmament programme had started.

Fortunately for Lockheed's, Hudson contracts for the RAF and subsequent orders for the Ventura bomber development of the Lodestar, together with big USAAF orders for the P-38 Lightning fighter, and large-scale production of the B-17F and B-17G Fortress, gave them a sufficient volume of military business to allow them to go ahead with the Constellation without fear of overstraining the company's resources, as it could conceivably have done in the

leaner years before 1938. As it turned out, the real worry was to be the extent to which demands on Lockheed for combat aircraft production would slow down the rate at which Constellations could be delivered to the airlines.

Construction of the prototype had started in 1940 to an initial order from TWA for nine Constellations, but Pan American Airways became interested in the design and on 11 June 1940 placed an order for no less than forty of a transoceanic variant designated Model 149, the largest order to date for one of the new four-engined transports, whereupon TWA soon increased its own order to forty. Both orders, however, had to be regarded as provisional after America's entry into the war and, in the event, Pan Am reduced its Constellation commitment after 1945 in favour of a fleet of Boeing Stratocruisers, but, even so, the orders do illustrate the benefits to a manufacturer of a large home

Multi-millionaire Howard Hughes, major shareholder in TWA, Hollywood impressario, record-breaking pilot and aircraft constructor, at the controls of a TWA Model 049 Constellation

market, and the extent to which airline competition stimulates transport aircraft design. Within the space of four years TWA had helped to sponsor, either alone or with other airlines, three new four-engined airliners, two of which, the DC-4 and Constellation and their developments, were to dominate the transport aircraft markets until turboprop and jet types arrived on the scene.

In 1941 a long-range heavy-bomber derivative of the Constellation, known to Lockheed as the Model 51, was prepared as a project for the United States Army Air Force (USAAF) in competition with the Boeing B-29 Superfortress, the Douglas XB-31 project and the Convair B-32 Dominator. Designated XB-30, the Lockheed entry had accommodation for a crew of twelve, a wing span of 123ft, a length of 104ft 8in and was powered by four 2,200hp Wright Duplex Cyclone R-3350-13 radials. The Constellation wings and power plants were married to a new fuselage, and the XB-30's estimated maximum speed was 382mph and its gross weight was 94,000lb; the Model 151 was a slightly different version, and the XB-30 was also known to Lockheed as the Model 249. In the end, the Boeing B-29 won this design competition and went into large-scale production, and the XB-30 did not get beyond the project stage.

In the same month that Constellation design started TWA's destinies were to come under the influence— not always beneficial—of a new principal stockholder, the enigmatic and controversial Howard Hughes. Heir to the multi-million dollar Hughes Tool Co, makers of oil-drilling rig machinery, of which he was to become the sole owner, Hughes had a deep and abiding interest in aviation, and some notable achievements to his credit as a designer-pilot. In 1935 he had set up a world record of 352mph with the Hughes H-1 racing aircraft designed by himself, and two years later established a US transcontinental flying record of 7hr 28min. In 1938 he and four others made a record-breaking round-the-world flight in a Lockheed 14, NX13973, starting from New York on July 10 and flying on to Paris, Moscow, across Siberia via Omsk and Yakutsk to Fairbanks (Alaska) and back to New York in 91hr 14min. He had also hit the public eye as a Hollywood impresario, directing the United Artists' spectacular 'Hells Angels' in 1931, and as the sponsor of film stars Jean Harlow and Jane Russell. He was an influence on the Constellation project from the begin-

ning, and in 1938 he acquired a financial stake in TWA, previously controlled by the Lehman financial interests in New York, when Jack Frye, then the airline's president, was seeking fresh capital. Early in 1947, after the airline had lost money heavily, Frye and Hughes came to a parting of the ways, Frye's resignation allegedly being prompted by Hughes (who then held 46 per cent of TWA's stock) insisting upon a change of management as a condition for helping to re-finance the airline.

Meanwhile the Constellation design was going ahead. The new project had a wing span of 123ft and a wing area of 1,650sq ft, the flush-riveted, stressed skin wing being basically a scaled-up version of the P-38 Lightning's, but with two main spars and a false spar carrying ailerons and flaps, instead of the P-38's single spar; the Lockheed-Fowler area-increasing flaps were similar to those first used on the Model 14, and gave an effective maximum lift coefficient of about 2·6 when extended, there being settings for take-off, landing and manoeuvring. The wing was built in seven sections: the centre section, the inner wings carrying the engine nacelles, the outer wings and detachable wing tips. Integral wing tankage for 4,000 US gal of fuel was provided in the Model L-049, the wing section being NACA-23 series, of 18 per cent thickness at the root tapering to 12 per cent (NACA 4412) at the tip. Maximum gross weight was to be 59,200lb when the project started, but increased to 68,000lb, resulting in a wing loading of 41lb per sq ft, though these figures were considerably higher for the first production aircraft. Hydraulic power-boosted controls with manual override were featured as well as thermal de-icing of the wing, tailplane and fin leading edges. The latter feature had been tested by the National Advisory Committee for Aeronautics (NACA) on a Lockheed 12A in 1940; serialled NACA 97, this had been fitted with at least two different types of third, central fin and used for lateral stability tests as well as de-icing trials. The Constellation tail unit was a scaled-up version of those of the Lockheed 12A and 14 with the addition of a third, central fin and rudder; tailplane span was 50ft and the elevators were metal-covered, although the rudders on the L-049 were fabric-covered.

Unlike that of the DC-4, which was a parallel-section tube, the Constellation's fuselage, of circular cross-section throughout its length, featured a

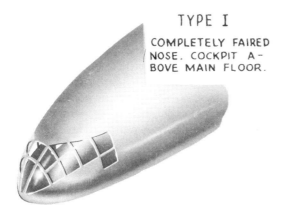

TYPE I
COMPLETELY FAIRED
NOSE. COCKPIT A-
BOVE MAIN FLOOR.

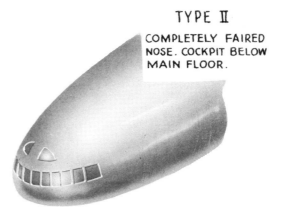

TYPE II
COMPLETELY FAIRED
NOSE. COCKPIT BELOW
MAIN FLOOR.

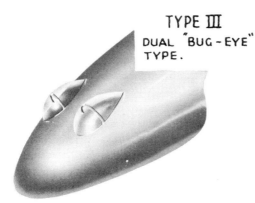

TYPE III
DUAL "BUG-EYE"
TYPE.

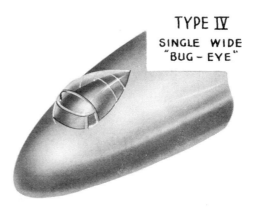

TYPE IV
SINGLE WIDE
"BUG-EYE"

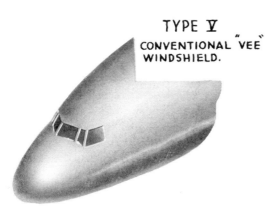

TYPE V
CONVENTIONAL "VEE"
WINDSHIELD.

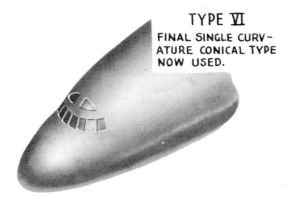

TYPE VI
FINAL SINGLE CURV-
ATURE CONICAL TYPE
NOW USED.

*The various windscreen/cockpit configurations studied in
the initial design stages*

cambered centre-line to give it an aerofoil-like profile in side view. This served both to increase the maximum width of level floor, especially in the nose and tail sections, and to shorten the nosewheel leg by 'drooping' the front fuselage, undercarriage height being dictated by the large airscrew diameter. Lockheed publicity at the time made some play with the supposed aerodynamic advantages of the 'lifting fuselage' but although wind-tunnel tests did indicate some reduction in drag it is doubtful if it amounted to much, and this fuselage shape has been criticised on the score that it prevents full utilisation of the interior space. Its use in the Constellation is an isolated example, and almost all major transport aircraft which followed retained the Douglas parallel-section fuselage—including Lockheed's own Electra turboprop which succeeded the Super Constellation series in production. The Constellation's maximum internal diameter of 132in allowed space for four-abreast seating in 22in-wide seats on either side of a 24-in aisle; later on, five-abreast seating for the higher density coach/economy layouts was to be adopted.

The Excalibur project had featured a conventional stepped windscreen but, doubtless inspired by the Boeing 307 Stratoliner, whose well-streamlined nose

Known as 'Sweater Girl' or 'Ven-tellation', this Ventura was fitted with two Wright R-3350-35s as an engine test-bed

shape eliminated the windscreen step, Lockheed studied several windscreen/cockpit configurations to eliminate, if possible, the drag of a step. The first of these was a completely faired nose with transparent glazing, but when it was mocked-up vision for the pilots was found to be bad. The second, also a completely faired nose, this time put the cockpit below the main floor, and was discarded because of its unsuitability for a belly landing or ditching, and also because of the extra drag produced by the larger nose. The third arrangement comprised two small 'bug eyes' for the pilot and co-pilot, a layout which Douglas tried after the war in the C-74 Globemaster, but this was found too claustrophobic for pilots on long flights, as well as creating problems in instrument layout and causing increased drag. The next attempt at a solution was to place both pilots together under a single large 'bug eye' but this again increased drag and introduced pressurisation difficulties. A conventional 'Vee-type' windscreen was also considered but the fuselage was too wide to allow of an effective design, and the idea was discarded in favour of the final solution, a windscreen with many small panels that gave vision angles equal to those on a DC-3 and involved the least weight penalty. There was a direct-opening panel for clear vision and an experimental de-icing system was tried, using infra-red rays.

In spite of the fuselage droop the Constellation's

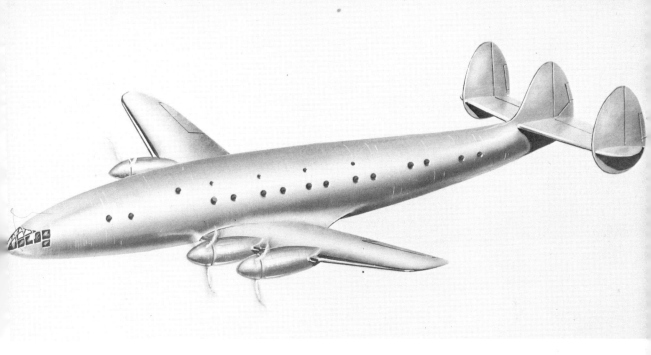

nosewheel leg is still a very long one (about 9ft 6in) and, unlike those of most later transports in the 1950s, retracted backwards, necessitating an electrically-driven stand-by pump for emergency extension instead of relying on the slipstream-assisted free-fall gravity method. Cabin pressure differential was $4\frac{1}{4}$lb/sq in, giving a cabin altitude of 8,000ft at a height of 20,000ft, there being two fully-automatic cabin superchargers with manual override control, either of which could maintain the correct air density. Cabin temperature was thermostatically controlled, a refrigeration unit cooling the cabin to 78° F when the outside temperature was 110° F. The undercarriage had dual wheels on all units, the main wheels, with low-pressure tyres, being carried on single shock-absorber struts retracting forwards behind twin doors into the engine nacelles. The steerable twin nosewheel was carried on a single shock-absorber leg with a fairing plate attached to its front which also retracted through twin doors. Dual hydraulic brakes were fitted to the main wheels.

The Model L-049 Constellation's four Wright R-3350 Duplex Cyclone engines gave it some 25 per cent more power than the Douglas DC-4, resulting in a higher speed, longer range and greater payload, not to mention operating costs per seat-mile some 23 per cent cheaper than those of the DC-4.

A Lockheed Ventura had been used as a flying test-bed for the R-3350 engines and this was known as the 'Ven-tellation' to Lockheed engineers when fitted with two 2,200hp R-3350-35s, and also as the 'Sweater Girl'. It was found to have a very similar performance to the Constellation, which made it especially useful for the latter's test programme, and when this was completed Lockheed sold it to the Wright Aeronautical Corporation for further engine development.

In order to achieve the lowest possible drag, the original Constellation nacelle design had featured a completely enclosed engine with a cooling air intake at the nacelle/wing juncture, the air being turned through 180 degrees to move forward to the front of the nacelle, where it turned through another 180 degrees to circulate through the cylinder fins. These duct bends produced losses, however, and wind-tunnel tests showed that the drag saving over a conventional nacelle with the cooling air inlet at the front was negligible. A very similar low-drag cooling system to the one studied by Lockheed's was employed on the de Havilland D.H. 91 Albatross airliner, which first flew on 20 May 1937, powered by four 535hp D.H. Gipsy Twelve 12-cylinder inverted-vee engines in low-drag nacelles.

Clarence L. 'Kelly' Johnson (left), chief research engineer and Milo Burcham, chief test pilot, in front of the Constellation prototype NX25800, which was painted dark green all over with grey under-surfaces and USAAF insignia

The R-3350s in the Constellation are enclosed in long-chord tapered cowlings, the stainless steel nacelles being completely detachable. They can be changed in thirty minutes, all ducting and controls being grouped at the fireproof bulkhead. In the early models the flight engineer operated the fire extinguisher system on activation of the fire-warning signal. Three-blade reversible pitch and fully-feathering Hamilton Standard Hydromatic or Curtiss Electric airscrews of 15ft 2in diameter are fitted. The Constellation was the first airliner with the ability to use reverse pitch and this feature has greatly reduced runway overrun accidents over the years, as well as facilitating operation from wet or icy surfaces.

The flight deck was initially laid out for a crew of five: two pilots with dual controls, a flight engineer's station to starboard behind the co-pilot and facing outward, a radio operator's position behind the pilot facing forward, and a navigator's position and crew rest space separated from the flight deck proper by a bulkhead. This layout underwent some revision over the years, notably with the disappearance of the flight engineer and radio officer from airline crews by the 1960s in favour of an all-pilot complement.

Cabin interiors also underwent considerable changes, reflecting the needs of different airlines, types of traffic and routes. Initially, Lockheed offered a variety of interiors seating up to sixty-four passengers by day, or twenty berths plus four seats in a sleeper version, with toilets, cloakroom and galley space abaft the seating area, while a lounge space, buffet or galley area could also be arranged at the front of the cabin behind the first-class seating or the flight deck. The main passenger entrance door is aft on the port side, with a crew entry door forward and to starboard. The two underfloor freight holds have a total capacity of 434cu ft.

The Prototype Flies

During 1941 and 1942 construction of the prototype went ahead as fast as Lockheed's military aircraft commitments would permit and on 9 January 1943, bearing the registration NX25800, it made its first flight from Lockheed's airfield at Burbank, California, piloted by Edmund T. (Eddie) Allen and Milo Burcham. The latter, who was killed in July 1944 while testing the Lockheed P-80 Shooting Star second prototype, was Lockheed's chief test pilot, while Allen, on temporary loan to Lockheed, held a similar appointment with Boeing. Also on board for the first flight were C. L. 'Kelly' Johnson, Lockheed's chief research engineer,

Rudy Thoren, assistant to Johnson, and chief mechanic Dick Stanton. Altogether, six flights were made that day, three by Milo Burcham and three by Eddie Allen, the latter summing up the general satisfaction with the new transport by saying, 'This thing works so perfect you don't need me around here any more'. Allen was killed less than six weeks later when the Boeing B-29 Superfortress prototype crashed.

After the first flight of one hour, during which the undercarriage was left down as a precautionary measure, the prototype was landed at the USAAF base at Muroc Field (now Edwards Air Force Base). The maximum gross weight, initially 68,000lb, had been increased during the design stages to 72,000lb, then to 77,050lb and finally to 86,250lb by the time the prototype first flew, and flight testing soon showed that the landing weight could be increased from 70,000lb to 75,000lb. The flight test programme progressed smoothly, the prototype flying with up to 8·8 tons of water ballast in tanks in the cabin (filled by a 4in-diameter fire hose) to simulate various loads and their effect at different centre of gravity positions. The essential soundness of the Constellation design was demonstrated by the fact that few modifications of any note were incorporated into the production aircraft as a result of flight tests, despite the design's many advanced technical features.

At one stage the hydraulic power boost for the controls was found to be rather too sensitive, but the trouble was soon corrected, and the Constellation was the first transport to go into production with power-boosted controls. This system was designed before stick-force criteria had been established by NACA or the US armed services, and Lockheed conducted its own survey to determine the forces that would be most acceptable to pilots: these were finally set at 50–80lb on the elevator, 150lb on the rudder pedal and 10ft–lb on each aileron. The amount of stick force required under the most critical control conditions for each control surface was then determined and a wide variety of boost systems and ratios were investigated. The final boost ratios were 9·33:1 for the elevators (ie the pilot's effort on the stick is multiplied 9·33 times by the boost system), 23:1 for the rudders and 26:1 for the ailerons. The prototype featured microswitches on the nose-wheel leg to check the loads upon it and a retractable tail skid under the rear fuselage for tail-down landings, and this was retained on production aircraft.

The first-ever Atlantic crossing by a Constellation was made by C-69C-1-LO 42-94550, seen here taxying in at Orly airport, when it flew non-stop from New York to Paris on 4 August 1945 in the record time of 14hr 12min

C-69-5-LO 42-94558 was used to test the Speedpak freight container

Flight tests of the prototype showed the Constellation to have an outstanding performance: its top speed of 347mph was faster than any four-engined bomber then in service and comparable with the cruising speeds of contemporary fighters. It met the design goal of one mile per gallon fuel consumption at the high cruising speed of 275mph on only 52·5 per cent power—a good deal faster than most other airliners cruised—while the payload for the design range proved much greater than originally estimated, and the original design specifications were met or exceeded in all respects. In addition its ample power reserves gave it a very good engine-out performance; it was designed to fly at 15,000ft with two engines stopped.

The Lockheed C-69

After the Pearl Harbour disaster, both TWA and Pan American had waived their rights to the Constellation in favour of the USAAF, which then took over the type under the designation C-69, the first production aircraft being completed as 63-seater troop transports. A proposed redesign of the C-69 for airline use of July 1943 was designated Model 449. Up to sixteen short tons of freight could also be carried although the C-69's freighting potential was limited by the fact that, unlike the Douglas C-54, it had no special freight doors. The war ended before any C-69 units could be formed, and the type did not see service in either the European or Pacific theatres of operations. Of the first production batch originally laid down for TWA at Burbank, twenty were completed for the

USAAF as C-69-1-LO and C-69-5-LO transports (Model L-49-10) and one as a C-69C-1-LO, the last two being C-69-10-LOs which had been allotted USAAF serials but were sold to TWA at the end of 1945 instead of going into military service. Of the remaining eighteen, four were sold to TWA after the war, having been refurbished to commercial standards, six went to BOAC and the rest to other operators, ultimately El Al (three) and Capital Airlines (two), except for one broken up, one that crashed at Topeka, Kansas, on 18 September 1945, following a nacelle fire, and one used as a static test airframe at Wright Field. The Topeka accident, in which the C-69 was being flown by a Pan American crew for USAAF Air Transport Command, resulted in all C-69s being temporarily grounded for modifications to the fuel system.

War surplus C-69s were sold off very cheaply, at least four for a mere $20,000 each, and two others went for only $40,000 apiece—an amazing bargain for a very modern and almost brand new four-engined airliner with only a few hundred hours flying time. By way of comparison, the selling price of Constellations built for the airlines in the early post-war years was to range up to $1,000,000 apiece.

The prototype was officially handed over to the USAAF on 28 July 1943 as a C-69-1-LO with the military serial 43-10309. The constructor's number was 1961 and it was later converted to the XC-69E-LO variant on being re-engined with four 2,100hp Pratt & Whitney Double Wasp R-2800-34 radials of the same type as fitted to the Douglas DC-6. Shortly after VJ Day in 1945, the prototype was declared surplus and was acquired by Howard Hughes from the US War Assets Administration at a sum believed to be only $40,000. It was sold without a certificate of air-worthiness, and was first re-registered NC25800, later becoming re-registered NX6700. From then until 1949, 'Old 1961', as it was later to be known to Lockheed employees after its constructor's number (which became 1961-S in L-1049 form), hardly flew at all, totalling less than 100 hours in the hands of Howard Hughes and his pilots. Early in 1950 Hughes sold it back to Lockheed for rebuilding into the L-1049 Super Constellation prototype.

Meanwhile, although all production was earmarked for the military, Jack Frye and Howard Hughes had given the travelling public a headline-catching fore-taste of post-war Constellation travel by flying the first production aircraft in TWA livery, carrying three other crew members and twelve passengers, from Burbank to Washington non-stop on 17 April 1944 in the record transcontinental time of 6hr, 57min, 30sec, the aircraft being handed over to the USAAF on arrival in Washington. Two more C-69s were delivered in October 1944, and almost all of the others at intervals through 1945, followed by a few in 1946. Sub-assembly and fabrication of Constellations was undertaken at Factory A adjoining the Lockheed Air Terminal at Burbank. This has been the plant of the former Vega Aircraft Corporation, formed in 1937 as an affiliate of Lockheed, which became a wholly-owned subsidiary in 1941 and was absorbed into Lockheed on 30 November 1943. Final assembly of Constellations was undertaken at the main Lockheed Factory B. By

Robert Gross, president of Lockheed (left) *and Jack Frye, TWA's president, after signing a Constellation contract*

1 January 1949 ten C-69s remaining on the USAF list (most of which had already been sold to civil operators) had been redesignated ZC-69 and ZC-69C, the 'Z' prefix denoting 'obsolete' status. Several more C-69 variants were projected but not built.

These were: C-69A (Model L-49-43-11) with accommodation for 100 troops and a crew of six.

C-69B (Model L-349) with accommodation for ninety-four troops on benches and a crew of six.

C-69C-1-LO (Model L-549) a personnel transport with accommodation for forty-three passengers in airline-type seats and a crew of six. One, serialled 42-94550, was delivered to the USAAF on 4 August 1945 and orders for forty-nine more were cancelled after VJ Day. The one delivered was given an experimental-category C of A as Model L-049-46-25 NX54212 and leased to TWA for pilot training from 10 June to 30 July 1946, and in March 1948 it was sold to BOAC as G-AKCE *Bedford*. Two more C-69 variants completed the series. These were:

C-69D project, orders for three of which were cancelled after VJ Day, with accommodation for sixty-three passengers and a crew of six;

XC-69E-LO, this being the designation of the prototype when re-engined with Double Wasp R-2800-34 radials for comparison as an alternative powerplant to the Duplex Cyclone R-3350s.

The aircraft started as C-69C and C-69D Constellations and cancelled after VJ Day, when most were at an early stage of construction, were completed as Model L-049s for the airlines, this being the first true commercial version which was certificated by the Civil Aeronautics Board (CAB) (Approved Type Certificate No. 763) on 11 December 1945 after only 27 hours of flight testing. With production under way, competition between Lockheed with the Constellation and Douglas with the DC-6 soon became intense, and was to continue as each manufacturer produced new and 'stretched' variants of the basic design. Yet the decision to go ahead with completion of the cancelled C-69s for the airlines, although apparently so logical, in fact involved big financial risks, even though it kept the work team together and enabled Lockheed to retain some 15,000 employees on their payroll after VJ Day, when most other aircraft firms were laying off men in their thousands. It was a gamble that was eventually to pay off handsomely, even though Lockheed's were to sustain heavy losses in 1946 and 1947.

2: Airline Service Begins

With the C-69 in production as a military transport, the end of World War II found Lockheed in a very strong position among long-haul airliner manufacturers. Even more than a year after the war's end the smaller, slower and unpressurised Douglas DC-4 was its most serious commercial rival, although design work had been going on at Santa Monica since 1944 on a 'stretched' and pressurised development with a 6ft 9in longer fuselage, powered by 2,100bhp Pratt & Whitney R-2800 Double Wasp radials. This was the DC-6, which made its first flight in military guise as the XC-112A on 15 February 1946 and entered commercial service with American Airlines on 27 April 1947, a year after the Constellation. So, for a while, Lockheed had the edge over Douglas, although the latter was in a much stronger position numerically in the four-engined field by virtue of the many war-surplus C-54s becoming available for conversion to civil use as DC-4s. No other European challengers were yet in sight, post-war four-engined British transport, such as the Avro Tudor and Handley Page Hermes, having proved to be uncompetitive with their US contemporaries.

National Airlines at first planned to order four Model 049s in 1945 for the New York–Miami route but chose DC-6s instead. This impression shows an 049 in National livery

Hostilities had hardly ceased before Lockheed was able to offer the first true commercial version, the Model L-49, later to be known as the L-049, to the airlines. Production aircraft had been started as C-69C and C-69D transports, but completed as L-049s, the designation L-049 covering those C-69s already completed that had been refurbished to commercial standards. The first Constellation to be built throughout as a commercial aeroplane was completed in 1947, and the 049—sixty-six of which were built plus seventeen more converted from C-69s—was intended equally for US domestic or long-haul overwater routes, whereas the later Model L-649 was designed mainly for the former and the L-749 largely for the latter. Certificated on 11 December 1945, the 049A's maximum gross weight was 90,000lb and landing weight 77,280lb initially, although in the 049D gross weight was increased to 96,000lb from November 1946 with minor structural alterations, made progressively through the Models 049B and 049C (see Table of Variants). Integral wing tankage for 4,000 US gal was provided in four tanks and the engines were commercial versions of the C-69's Wright R-3350-35s, designated R-3350-745C18BA-1 and giving 2,200bhp each for take-off.

Pan American began Constellation operations in January 1946; NC88832 is seen here with the letter 'C' of its registration taped over as 'X' to denote experimental status

Lockheed's Constellation designations comprised the basic model number followed by a second number indicating the variant of R-3350 installed and a third number indicating which Lockheed-designed cabin interior was featured. Thus the Model 649-84-21 was the domestic version with Wright GR-3350-749C18BD-1 radials and accommodation for thirty-eight passengers; the Model 749-79-22 was the intercontinental version with the same model R-3350s and with accommodation for forty-four passengers by day or twenty in sleeper berths for overnight stages, with four more in seats. The suffix '-12' denoted a 64-passenger interior for domestic routes with a crew of two pilots, a flight engineer and two stewardesses, while the suffix '-24' denoted a 50-passenger layout in which the seats of each second row could be reclined to convert to twenty-four sleeper seats or couchettes. This version carried a crew of four, including one stewardess.

By the end of 1945 Lockheed had orders for 103 Constellations, mostly L-049s, to a total value of some $75,500,000; besides Pan American and TWA, customers included American Export Airlines (which became American Overseas Airlines when it was taken over by American Airlines), Eastern Air Lines (which had ordered L-649s), Air France, KLM Royal Dutch Airlines, KNILM and Pan American Grace Airways (Panagra). Northwest Airlines—better known as

Northwest Orient—had planned to order five Constellations for its post-war fleet but, instead, chose Boeing Stratocruisers to supplement its DC-4s, while National Airlines of Miami, which had originally intended to order four for the 'plum' New York-Miami route, chose DC-6s instead. KLM's East Indies subsidiary KNILM did not go ahead with its order for four nor was Panagra's order for two proceeded with. TWA itself had originally planned a fleet of no less than fifty-nine Constellations for domestic and international routes in the first flush of enthusiasm for post-war traffic growth, but cut this back by thirty-seven aircraft when the US domestic air traffic bubble burst in 1946 and 1947. During this period US airline managements, faced by financial difficulties and rising costs, cancelled over half of the 610 airliners of post-war design they had on order.

The First Transatlantic Services
TWA had taken delivery of its first L-049 on 1 October 1945, this being followed by thirty more plus eight others bought secondhand, and began crew training and route proving for the new type, an Atlantic

TWA originally intended to operate Constellation services to China, but political considerations prevented this. Seen here is 049 N86516 Star of Ireland

proving flight between Washington and Paris being flown on 3/4 December by Constellation NC86505, named *Paris Sky Chief* for the occasion, with twenty-three passengers on board. This flew via Gander (Newfoundland) and Shannon (Eire) to Orly Airport, covering the 3,870 miles in a total time of 12hr 57min at an average speed of 316mph. TWA began regular scheduled North Atlantic services on 5 February 1946 between New York and Paris with Model 049-46-26 NC86511 *Star of Paris*, piloted by Capt Harold F. Blackburn, and thirty-five passengers. Pan American, which had ordered twenty-two of these aircraft, had begun 049 Atlantic flights two weeks earlier, on 20 January, and flew its inaugural eastbound Atlantic flight to the UK on 4 February from New York's La Guardia to Hurn airport, near Bournemouth, then serving as the British transatlantic terminal until Heathrow was ready. Calls were made at Gander and Shannon and the aircraft, a Model 049-46-26 NC88833 named *Clipper Bald Eagle*, was commanded by Capt R. W. Fordyce and carried twenty-nine passengers. It returned to New York with a load of thirty-six passengers and two cabin staff in the 43-seat cabin, no sleeping-berths being fitted. At this early stage of Atlantic travel a number of passenger facilities were still lacking both in the air and on the ground; Hurn

airport, for instance, had no proper loading steps and its other terminal facilities were still decidedly spartan, while the Constellation itself had, as yet, no humidifier in its cabin pressurisation system.

Two days before TWA inaugurated its Paris service a Constellation piloted by the airline's president and founder, Jack Frye, made a record-breaking trans-continental flight with forty-five passengers to celebrate Lockheed's twentieth birthday, flying non-stop from Los Angeles to New York's La Guardia airport in 7hr, 27min and 48sec, covering the great circle course of 2,740 statute miles at an average height of 15,000ft and an average ground speed of 330mph. TWA began regular transcontinental services with the Constellation on 15 February 1946 between New York and Los Angeles, three weeks ahead of American Airlines which began DC-4 flights over this route on 7 March, followed by United shortly afterwards, also with DC-4s. With its two major transcontinental competitors having to operate the unpressurised and 80mph slower Douglas transport, TWA had a strong competitive lead with the Constellation and despite the type's grounding through engine troubles, this lead was maintained until the introduction of DC-6s by American Airlines and United a year later. The Constellation's superior speed and range enabled TWA to offer a one-stop New York–Los Angeles schedule of 9hr 45min eastbound and 11hr westbound, compared with American's two-stop DC-4 schedule via Washington and Dallas (Texas) taking 13hr 10min eastbound and 14hr 25min westbound.

American Airlines overcame this equipment disadvantage by scheduling more DC-4 flights, which in March 1947 totalled twelve daily compared with TWA's six, and so succeeded in holding its share of the market, carrying about 3,500 passengers between New York and Los Angeles in that month compared with TWA's total of about 3,300.

With the introduction of DC-6s by American Airlines and—from May 1947—by United, TWA's competitors were at less of a disadvantage and the traffic battle settled down to an even fight between TWA and American, with United trailing some way behind in terms of frequencies offered. In September 1947 TWA carried 37 per cent of the passengers on the New York–Los Angeles route, American 47 per cent and United 16 per cent. TWA also put Constellations on the New York-San Francisco route, at first with three stops at Chicago, Kansas City and Los Angeles, with a time comparable to United's DC-4s which made only one stop at Omaha (Nebraska). In May 1947 United inaugurated an overnight DC-6 flight on this route with no traffic stop taking 9hr 55min for the eastbound crossing, and TWA replied on 1 July by inaugurating a one-stop (at Chicago) Constellation overnight service to San Francisco taking 10hr 10min eastbound and 11hr 40min westbound. This, together with an improved service to and from San Francisco via Los Angeles, effectively met United's competition and also American's.

Meanwhile, other operators were putting Constellations into service on the Atlantic and other intercontinental routes. The Brazilian national carrier Panair do Brasil, formed as a subsidiary of Pan American and in which the latter still had a 48 per cent holding, started operating regular Constellation services to London from Rio de Janeiro on 27 April 1946, calling at Dakar, Lisbon, Madrid and Paris. Panair's Constellations—the initial fleet was three—were acquired from Pan American, which eventually turned over sixteen 049s to the Brazilian carrier, and on 16 April one of these, PP-PCF *Manoël de Borba Gato*, landed at London's newly-opened Heathrow Airport on a proving flight with fourteen passengers. It thus became the first of its type and, indeed, the first aircraft of a foreign airline to land at London Airport, as well as inaugurating the first Brazilian service to the United Kingdom. Panair's Constellations later extended their European routes to include Rome, Zurich, Frankfurt, Istanbul and Beirut, as well as operating the more important ones in South America, such as those to Santiago and Lima. On 20 December 1953 a Panair Constellation completed what was claimed to be the world's longest commercial flight when it flew non-stop between Lisbon and Rio de Janeiro, covering the 4,837 miles in 21hr 40min. The elegant shape of PP-PCF on the Heathrow apron that April afternoon was a foretaste of how much more international long-haul air transport was to become now that it was no longer (as before the war) solely in the hands of the USA and a few European countries.

American Overseas Airlines had been the first to operate a scheduled landplane service across the

American Overseas Airlines operated seven 049s—NC90922 Flagship Copenhagen *is seen here—on routes to Germany and Scandinavia*

Panair do Brasil 049 PP-PCF was formerly NC88849 of Pan American and one of sixteen acquired from the latter

Atlantic, beginning with a DC-4 crossing from New York to Hurn on 23–24 October 1945. AOA's sphere of influence was Germany and Scandinavia, including Finland and Iceland, as well as the UK, and on 23 June 1946 the first of a fleet of seven L-049-46-27s went into service on these routes, followed by eight Boeing Stratocruisers. But in those early post-war years there was not really enough traffic to support three US airlines on the Atlantic, and Pan Am, which had bitterly contested American Export Airlines' entry on this route in 1942, eagerly sought an opportunity to buy out or otherwise eliminate AOA. This eventually came about on 25 September 1950, after President Truman, despite TWA's protests, had given approval for Pan Am's acquisition of AOA, so reversing his previous endorsement of the CAB's rejection of this deal. AOA's fleet of Constellations was thereupon taken over by Pan Am.

Air France had meanwhile taken delivery of four 049 Constellations, in June 1946, chiefly for the Paris–New York route on which they began services on 24 June, but the French airline's main commitment was to the L-749 and L-749A for expanding its routes to Africa, the Far East and South America. The four 049s were sold to TWA in January and February 1950, following Air France's purchase in December of an equal number of 749-79-46 Constellations from Pan American, which had bought these aircraft to provide

extra capacity pending the delivery of its Strato-cruisers; Air France had already taken delivery of about half of its L-749s on order.

KLM Royal Dutch Airlines ordered six Model 049s for its long-haul routes from Amsterdam, particularly to New York and to Batavia (shortly to become Djakarta with Indonesian independence) and took delivery of the first, PH-TAU *Utrecht*, on 28 May 1946. KLM had actually placed provisional orders for four Constellations and four DC-4s in 1943, while the war was still on, even though Lockheed could not at this time supply Connies to the airlines. One crashed at Prestwick on 28 October 1948, three were sold to Capital Airlines Inc in the summer of 1950 when they were replaced by 749s, and the remaining two were acquired by TWA. By 1950 Capital had become the fifth largest US domestic airline in terms of passengers carried and its ex-KLM Constellations joined two other converted C-69s on the more important of Capital's routes in the north-east United States, remaining the airline's first-line equipment until displaced by the Vickers Viscount fleet ordered in 1954, together with some more L-749s acquired from KLM. Capital's 049Es featured a 'Cloud Club Room' lounge forward with seating for eight people, and four-abreast seating for fifty-six passengers in the main cabin, and remained in service until 1960.

A more unusual and exotic interior was featured on the three Model L-049E Constellations of Cia Cubana de Aviacion SA acquired from Pan American, of which Cubana was a wholly-owned subsidiary before the war and in which Pan Am still had a sizeable holding. The Cuban airline had started a Havana–Mexico City Constellation service on 17 September 1953, and later put these aircraft on to a number of other routes, including Havana–Miami. In 1956 a new management headed by 33-year old Juan M. Palli Diaz, formerly vice-president and general manager, took over and it was he who suggested that artists from Havana's world-famous Tropicana night club be engaged to help boost load factors on the Thursday evening Havana–Miami Constellation flight, Cubana having lost traffic on this route to other airlines with more modern aircraft to such an extent that more than fifteen passengers each way was considered a good load. Top artists from the Tropicana were hired, a baby grand piano was fitted in the forward part of the cabin and the service was named 'The Tropicana Express'. The night club act, complete with drums as well as the piano, was temporarily successful in winning back some of the lost traffic until Viscounts took over the Havana–Miami route in August 1956. Another Latin American operator of 049s was the Venezuelan airline, Linea Aeropostal Venezolana, which took delivery of two on 31 October 1946, followed by two 749s a year later; with these, a direct Caracas–New York service was inaugurated on 21 March 1947, followed by other regional routes in the Caribbean area and, in October 1953, a service to Rome via the Azores, Lisbon and Madrid. LAV's two 049s were sold to Braniff in August 1955.

Controversy Over BOAC Order

But of all the post-war orders for Constellations probably none aroused more controversy in their respective countries than BOAC's order for five Model 049-46-25s, announced to the House of Commons on 24 January 1946 by the Parliamentary Secretary to the Ministry of Civil Aviation. To both aviation people and the general public the order came as a considerable shock, and several prominent aviation personalities expressed themselves forcibly about it. To the British public, with strong belief in the notable war-winning qualities of such aircraft as the Avro Lancaster and de Havilland Mosquito, the Constellation purchase seemed a retrograde step, especially at a time of dollar shortage, and fuel was added to the fire when, a few months later, BOAC ordered six Boeing Stratocruisers. As *The Aeroplane* of 6 September 1946 commented in its editorial:

> As we have frequently pointed out in this paper, if, three years ago, when the Brabazon Committee was planning our production, four Bristol Centaurus engines had been taken and a trans-Atlantic liner built around them, we should by now have a British type larger than the Constellation and not much smaller than the Stratocruiser. But the Powers That Be knew better, so what alternative is there to the present policy if we are not to lose most of our Atlantic traffic to the Americans?

And *The Aeroplane Spotter* for 4 May 1946 carried two large photos of Constellations on its front page

One of three 049s acquired from KLM in 1950, N86531 Capitaliner United States was previously PH-TAU Utrecht

Allotted the Panamanian registration RX-121, El Al's 049 N90827 later became 4X-AKA

and underneath these lines from Walt Whitman's 'Song of the Open Road':

The earth, that is sufficient,
   I do not want the constellations any nearer,
I know they are very well where they are,
   I know they suffice for those who belong to them

Yet BOAC's Constellation order could be defended far more easily than several of its later purchases of American types, for at that time there was really no alternative if the Corporation's competitive position on the Atlantic was to be maintained. The Avro Tudor I originally intended for this route—and the Constellations were at first envisaged as 'interim' equipment until the Tudors were ready—had accommodation for only twelve passengers and would have been much too small to have remained competitive.

In January 1947 the Ministry of Supply in London issued draft specification 2/47 for a medium-range Empire airliner, and ten companies tendered designs. Among them was the Bristol Aeroplane Co, which offered the Type 175. This was the aeroplane which was later to emerge as the Britannia with Bristol Proteus turboprops, although the Type 175 at that stage was a 32-passenger aeroplane with four Bristol Centaurus 662 or 663 radials, and smaller than the Britannia that eventually appeared. But it is interesting to note that Bristol had concluded that the 2/47 specification could best be met by building the Constellation under licence in this country with Bristol Centaurus 662 engines, a scheme which became known as Project Y. Lockheed would have been willing to grant a licence and it was considered that British-built Constellations could have been available at about the

same time and for the same price as the Type 175s. Bristol had also had some discussions with Lockheed as to the possibility of fitting Bristol Centaurus engines in five Model L-749s which BOAC might also purchase, this scheme being known, somewhat sinisterly, as Project X. In the end, sanction was refused for further dollar expenditure and Projects X and Y were both abandoned while the Type 175 design went ahead.

The first of ten BOAC Constellation proving flights to London's Heathrow airport from New York was flown on 16 June 1946 by G-AHEM *Balmoral* with Capt W. S. May in command, in the record time of 11hr 24min non-stop. Regular services to New York began on 1 July, twice-weekly at first, soon stepped up to three a week, and then a daily flight. BOAC's 049s were later put on to other routes and remained in service until the Comet accidents early in 1954 forced BOAC to take drastic measures to restore the capacity lost by the withdrawal of the de Havilland jet. More Stratocruisers had to be ordered and the seven L-049Es then in service (two more ex-AOA 049s had been acquired from Pan American early in 1953 and a converted C-69C had been bought in March 1948) were exchanged with Capital Airlines in return for seven of the latter's L-749A-79-24s which, with their higher gross weight, had the improved payload/range which was now needed for the Commonwealth routes. The deal, which enabled BOAC to standardise its fleet with the later model Constellations, involved a cash adjustment payment to Capital Airlines of £1,375,000. BOAC also had the expense of refurbishing the newly-acquired Capital aircraft to its own standards, this work including a change of cabin interior, galleys and associated fittings and the installation of long-range radio. The first ex-BOAC L-049E to leave the UK on delivery to Capital was G-AHEM *Balmoral*, which departed on 8 October 1954, and the seventh was handed over to the US airline at the end of June 1955.

It may be noted here that the designation L-049E was applied from 1953 to the L-049 with maximum all-up weight increased from 96,000lb to 98,000lb. Of the original five BOAC 049s one, G-AHEN *Baltimore*, was damaged in a crash at Filton, Bristol on 8 January 1951. It was written off, bought by Mel Adams & Associates, and shipped as deck cargo to the USA where it was rebuilt by Lockheed Air Services International at New York's Idlewild airport using parts of C-69-1-LO 43-10314 (constructor's number: 1966). It was registered N74192 and on completion of the rebuild was sold to California Hawaiian Airlines Inc, a US charter operator or 'non sked' that specialised in holiday charters to Hawaii. In September 1953 it was sold to El Al Israel Airlines as 4X-AKD, and the Israeli airline fitted it out to seat sixty-three tourist-class passengers, besides making some changes in the cockpit instrumentation and installing a new cargo compartment.

Grounding Through Engine Troubles

Although the Constellation was firmly established on the international scene by mid-1946 it was not without its troubles, and fires in the Wright R-3350 engines were a particular problem. Following an engine fire in a Pan American 049 in June 1946, the CAB issued a ruling that the cabin supercharger drive shafts from the outer engines must be disconnected and sealed off. This meant that the aircraft had temporarily to be operated unpressurised, flying at lower altitudes, and without

the cabin heating supplied by two superchargers to a pair of Janitrol-type heaters under the cabin floor. These drive shafts, taken from the two outer engines, were about 2ft long, each supercharger being mounted adjacent to the engine, and the troubles arose from the vibration transmitted from the flexibly-mounted engines. The R-3350s had also suffered a number of fires in the induction system, a problem separate from the supercharger drive, and this was finally solved by the installation of direct fuel injection to the engines, although a Bendix direct cylinder fuel injection system had also been available for the Wright R-3350 for some time previously as an alternative.

Following the crash of TWA 049 NC86513 on 11 July 1946 in a hayfield near TWA's training base at Reading, Pennsylvania, after a fire in No 3 engine, the CAB grounded all Constellations, and the type remained grounded until 23 August at a cost of about $50,000,000 for the fifty-eight aircraft involved. Tests continued to find the cause of this training flight crash, in which all but one of the five crew were killed, and also the cause of the repeated engine fires; there had been 46 cases of trouble with the cabin supercharger drive up to the Pan American 049 fire which had led to its being disconnected. A Constellation had been fitted in May 1946 with direct injection fuel feeds in place of the Bendix-Stromberg injection carburetters in its R-3350s and two-speed

One of five 049s bought by Modern Air Transport from Capital in 1961, N86533 was, after sale by the former, impounded at Asuncion after a smuggling flight

N88868, seen here, was one of four 049s and 149s acquired by American Flyers from Delta Air Lines in 1960

superchargers instead of single-speed ones. This commenced a 100hr programme of test flying to prove this new fuel distribution system, which eliminated the carburetter, and thus the seat of induction fires caused by blow-backs, in favour of injecting the fuel into the eye of the supercharger. This also had the advantage of eliminating carburetter freezing. Although the R-3350 had given excellent service mechanically the induction distribution had never been entirely satisfactory. To solve this problem, Lockheed test flew a Constellation with one engine fitted with spark plugs in various parts of the induction system so that fires could be started at will, and the system's susceptibility to fires investigated. About 150 fires were started on this engine for test purposes and all were successfully extinguished without using the main extinguisher system and without the aircraft being hazarded. A month or two prior to the grounding, modifications had been approved to the cabin supercharger drive shaft and to the supercharger lubrication system and bearings; several aircraft had been thus modified before the Pan American fire in June, after which some further mods to the drive shaft were approved. The enquiry into the Reading accident concluded that the fire originated as a result of a fault

in the electrical system, and the CAB ordered thirty-seven minor modifications to be made to the Constellation, mainly to the electrical system. Direct injection was not specifically required by the CAB although it had now become a standard feature on all Constellations, and those not so fitted were being modified retrospectively at the time of the Reading accident.

The engines with direct injection were designated R-3350-745C18BA-3, and at first one and then all of BOAC's 049s were fitted with the new fuel distribution system. Pan American also fitted its 049s and 749s with a new type of engine analyser that made possible detection and visual presentation of engine faults while airborne, being the first airline to fit its aircraft with such a device. And following the forced landing of Pan Am's 049 NC88845 *Clipper Eclipse* in Syria on 19 June 1947 after No 2 engine had caught fire and fallen out of the aircraft, it was recommended that methyl bromide be used in place of CO_2 in the fire extinguisher system. Pan Am's 049 NC88856 *Clipper Paul Jones* was also fitted with an experimental periscopic sextant for the navigator instead of the drag-producing astrodome.

The Israeli Constellations

The three Model 049s delivered to El Al Israel Airlines in the summer of 1950 came to normal airline service by a devious and incident-filled route in which intrigue and a certain amount of deception were not lacking. They had been acquired (together with a fourth) in 1947 and 1948 as surplus C-69s from the USAF by a non-scheduled US operator, Intercontinental Airways, formed by Mr Al Schwimmer, a former TWA flight engineer with Zionist sympathies, who had also formed the Schwimmer Aviation Corporation in 1947 to operate Constellation freight services between the USA and Europe. The state of Israel had been proclaimed on 14 May 1948 and it was immediately fighting a war of independence with neighbouring Arab states to establish and assert its identity.

The US State Department and Great Britain imposed an embargo on the supply of arms to Israel, and transport aircraft which could be used for military purposes as well as combat aircraft, both badly needed by the new state in its struggle for survival, came under this ban. This did not, however, prevent a number of attempts by those sympathetic to the Jewish cause to get round the ban and supply the much-needed aircraft. The three Constellations that ultimately went into El Al service were registered with a Panamanian airline, Lineas Aereas de Panama SA, and, although nominally Panamanian, flew supplies into Israel from Prague and other places for some months with the Israeli Air Force Transport Command. Al Schwimmer and two other pilots, Sam Lewis and Les Gardner, had planned to evade the arms embargo and fly ten Curtiss C-46s and the three Constellations out of the USA to Israel in 1948. But after the ten C-46s had been flown out and ferried to Lydda the US authorities ordered the three 049s, which were waiting at Milville, New Jersey, to be impounded. However, Sam Lewis managed to take-off with one of them and this later damaged its undercarriage in Czechoslovakia on 9 June 1949, but was repaired. Later still it crashed on

the seashore about a quarter of a mile short of the Tel Aviv airstrip while attempting an emergency landing. It was subsequently repaired in California and refurbished for El Al's use. The other two 049s remained in the States for a time and Schwimmer, Gardner and Lewis were arrested and tried on charges of 'conspiracy to violate the Neutrality Act and Export Control Law'. Lewis was acquitted but the other two were convicted and fined $10,000 each. Lineas Aereas de Panama's route licences had been bought by Schwimmer and his associates and one of the 049s, N90829, which became 4X-AKC, did actually appear in this airline's livery late in 1949 but it is unlikely that any of the 049s ever actually operated into Panama.

The three 049s were sold to El Al in June 1950 and were converted at Burbank to Model L-249 standard, this being almost the same as a Model 649 and with a maximum gross weight of 100,000lb. The interiors were completely refurbished and the flight-deck layout considerably changed. Accommodation for the relief crew was reduced to enable more passenger seats to be fitted, one layout seating up to eighty-five passengers, and others sixty or sixty-six; a 63-seat interior was standardised in 1954 and a 58-seat version for the Tel Aviv–Johannesburg and New York routes in 1955. Speedpak cargo containers were bought second-hand for use on the European routes. El Al's 049s inaugurated a Tel Aviv–London–New York service on 16 May 1951, besides taking over the Johannesburg route and replacing the airline's DC-4s on the European routes. On 27 July 1955, 4X-AKC was shot down by Bulgarian jet fighters near the frontier with

Ex-TWA 049 N90831 in service with Air Belize International (left) *and Lake Havasu City (Lake Havasu Airlines)*

Used aircraft dealers, as well as airlines, had their names on some of the aircraft they owned, as shown by this ex-TWA 049 in the livery of Dellair

Sales to Non-scheduled Carriers

A number of TWA 049s were leased to Eastern Air Lines in the winter seasons of 1956–57 and 1957–58 for the Florida holiday traffic. TWA retired its 049s at the end of 1961 and sold twenty-five of them to the Nevada Airmotive Corporation on 31 March 1962, a few more being sold direct to other airlines. During the early 1960s they were acquired, usually on lease from Nevada Airmotive, by a number of the smaller US non-scheduled carriers, who found the 049 a cheap and capacious aircraft for charter work, combining low first cost with a seating capacity of around eighty and good spares backing. The US 'non-skeds' which acquired 049s sold off by TWA and other carriers included Coastal Cargo Coastal Air Lines, American Flyers Airline Corp, Imperial Airlines, Magic City Airways, Futura Air Lines, Standard Airways, Consolidated Airlines, World Wide Airlines, Modern Air Transport, ASA International Airlines (a scheduled freight carrier), Edde Airlines, Hawthorne Nevada Airlines, Pacific Air Transport and Paradise Airlines. To operators like Modern Air Transport, with five ex-Capital 049s, and American Flyers, which bought two 049s and two L-149s from Delta Air Lines on 1 April 1960, these Constellation fleets were often their first four-engined equipment and an important stage towards eventual acquisition of jets. But two other 049 operators, Imperial and Paradise, both went out of business after suffering an accident with the type; Paradise had specialised in flying holidaymakers to the Nevada ski resorts.

An ex-Braniff Model 049 acquired by the US 'non-sked' Lloyd Airlines was impounded by the Bolivian authorities at Santa Cruz de la Sierra on

Greece, while on a flight from Vienna to Tel Aviv, with the loss of all fifty-one passengers and seven crew. The Israeli Government protested strongly but it was not until several years later that a marginal sum in compensation was paid.

Two more 049s were acquired by El Al from Cubana in October 1955, although, in the end, only one was delivered and given an extensive overhaul, including flight deck and cabin interior modifications, to bring it to the same standard as the other 049s. From December 1957 El Al's Britannia 313s began to take over as first-line equipment but it was not until 1962 that the last three Constellations in service were sold to Universal Sky Tours Ltd, principal shareholders in Euravia (London) Ltd, which later became Britannia Airways. Sky Tours started 049 operations on 5 May 1962, specialising in the group charter and inclusive tour market.

As TWA took delivery of its L-749s and, later, Super Constellations, its Model 049s were turned over more and more to coach-class domestic services, which had been started early in 1950 with three L-749s seating eighty-one passengers. By 1958 most of TWA's thirty-two 049s had 81-seater coach-class interiors, although some 57-seaters were retained for first-class domestic services. The original 47-passenger layout for the Atlantic had later been superseded by a 60-seat tourist-class interior for this route, and another layout for thirty-two passengers in reclining seats was for a time featured for 'Sleeper Seat' services on international routes.

ASA International Airlines (Aerovias Sud Americana Inc) leased three ex-TWA 049s, including N86506 seen here, in 1962

2 August 1961 on suspicion of smuggling while engaged on a charter flight from Miami to Uruguay. A Bolivian Air Force F-51D Mustang fighter was sent up to intercept it but the Constellation pilot took a shot at it through the open cockpit window with a revolver and, according to reports, forced the Mustang down! Lloyd ceased operations after this incident. One of Modern's 049s was sold to a Senor Rymar of Montevideo in June 1965 and leased to the International Carribean Corporation; it was impounded by the Paraguayan authorities at Asuncion on 9 September 1965, also for smuggling.

The four 049s which American Flyers had bought from Delta had been sold by Pan American to Delta on 1 February 1956 and in the latter's service two were converted to Model L-149s. This version was created by fitting the long-range wings of the Model L-749, whose fuel tanks had a total capacity of 5,820 US gal, to the Model 049 fuselage. Two of the smaller British independent airlines, Trans-European Aviation and Falcon Airways, operated 049s; the former had acquired one from Cubana but this was seized at Charlotte, North Carolina, on 27 January 1961 en route to the UK by a Mr Jacob Shapiro, who was claiming $750,000 in respect of a hosiery mill he had owned in Cuba and which had been appropriated by the Cuban Government. This 049 was never delivered, and Trans-European bought two of Falcon's three ex-Capital 049s. One of these was later impounded in Israel; the other was held at Gatwick for non-payment of landing fees before Trans-European went out of business in 1962. The same fate overtook Falcon, the managing director of which, Capt Marian Kozubski, was a colourful merchant-venturing character whose

career with Falcon and other airlines had included a number of brushes with airworthiness and safety authorities. He later acquired one of Euravia's ex-El Al 049s for Britair East African Airways, a Kenya-based charter operator. The Austrian charter operator, Aero Transport, acquired an ex-TWA 049 and later two L-749As. One of their Constellations was grounded at Djibouti in French Somaliland in November 1963 by the French authorities while carrying a cargo of arms for the Yemeni Royalists fighting the Egyptians, but their more usual sphere of operations was air charter holidays in Europe.

Another little-known territory to be served by 049 was the independent state of Burundi, previously part of the Belgian protectorate of Rwanda-Urundi, adjacent to the Congo. Royal Air Burundi, the national airline, started operations early in 1963, several non-scheduled flights being made between Usumbura, the then capital, and Europe with an ex-TWA 049 registered with Las Vegas Hacienda of Las Vegas, Nevada (the Hacienda Hotel), a US indirect air carrier and tour operator (as the CAB called it) which used several ex-TWA 049s to fly inclusive tour and holiday charter parties to Las Vegas from other parts of the States. Royal Air Burundi ceased operations after a few months, its one and only 049 being flown back to Oakland, California, in the summer of 1963. Several of the Las Vegas Hacienda 049s were later acquired by Lake Havasu City (Lake Havasu Airlines), owned by the firm that bought London Bridge to reopen it in Arizona, one of these being disposed of to another inclusive tour charter operator, Hawthorn Nevada Airlines, for a time in 1968, while two more were sold to Southeastern Skyways Inc in 1970. An ex-Paradise Airlines 049 was leased in 1966 to the Dominican operator Aerovias Nacionales Quisqueyanas for scheduled and charter services from Santo Domingo, and an ex-Capital 049 was acquired in August 1966 by the Chilean charter operator, Transportes Aereos Squella. Another Chilean carrier, Air Chile/Lyon Air or ALA—Sociedad de Transportes Aereos— had operated cutprice services at below IATA (International Air Transport Association) fares from Santiago up the west coast of South America to Havana with an 049 leased from Cubana during 1957–58.

Las Vegas Hacienda (the Hacienda Hotel) used N9412H and several other ex-TWA 049s to fly holidaymakers to Las Vegas

3: The Type is Developed

By the end of 1946 the Constellation was established on the international scene as an outstanding airliner, setting new standards of speed and comfort in international travel and giving TWA and Pan Am such a lead on the US domestic and Atlantic routes as to oblige other airlines, like BOAC and Air France, to order the type to retain their competitive positions. With the engine troubles that had caused the grounding now behind it—although, like any big radial of this horsepower, the R-3350 still demanded careful handling to get the best out of it—the Constellation could well face the competition of the DC-6s which were now coming off the production line at Santa Monica for United, American, Sabena, KLM and other operators. Weight growth and increased power were the two obvious avenues of Constellation development to which Lockheed had been turning their attention; the prototype's maximum gross weight had been 86,250lb and the 049's, originally certificated at 90,000lb, had soon gone up to 96,000lb and—with the 049E model—to 98,000lb. Indeed, it was weight growth rather than, as with the Douglas transports from DC-4 to DC-7C, fuselage growth that was to be the characteristic and recurrent theme of Constellation development. The Wright R-3350 was at the beginning of its commercial life and, a more recent and more powerful engine than the Pratt & Whitney R-2800 of the DC-6, offered greater potentialities for power increases. Indeed, Lockheed may be said to have pioneered with the Constellation the now common practice of airliner manufacturers in offering progressive increases in gross weight of the same basic model over a period of time, a practice which has really come to the fore with the thrust-growth potential of the modern jet engine.

One feature of the Constellation which might easily, in view of its advanced nature at that time, have given a lot of trouble was the hydraulic power-boost operation of the controls but, thanks to good design and careful rig testing before the prototype first flew, this did not prove to be a problem. The Constellation had exceptional controllability at all speeds, as well as excellent stall characteristics, and it was easy to maintain a heading at low speeds with one or both engines on one side stopped. This was convincingly demonstrated on 19 February 1947, when an Air France Constellation on the Atlantic route from New York to Paris flew over 600 miles to a landing at Casablanca with both starboard engines stopped. A faulty operation of the unit linking No 4 engine to its propeller had resulted in a major oil leak in the unit, which drained the engine's front section of oil and caused it to run dry. No 4 propeller windmilled after the engine had been stopped and, grinding on its hub, overheated and projected molten metal particles—luckily there was only a small oil fire. No 4 prop eventually broke from its shaft and hit No 3 engine, chopping off a sizeable portion of No 3 propeller's blades and damaging several cylinder heads, causing vibrations that ceased when No 3 propeller was feathered. The flight was continued on the two port engines operating at 1,250hp, and averaged 150mph to a safe landing at Casablanca. On another occasion a Pan Am 049, after a forced landing with engine trouble, was flown across the States to the west coast for repairs with the offending engine removed and replaced by a fairing.

The Model L-649 Constellation

As the war drew to a close the Wright company had been working out the improvements to the R-3350 that war experience, especially in the Boeing B-29 Superfortress, had shown to be necessary and were in a position to produce a new and truly commercial version of this engine. This became known as the GR-3350-749C18BD-1 and gave more power—2,500bhp for take-off—than the Model 049's power plants, as well as having direct fuel injection as standard. In May 1945 Lockheed began design work on the Model L-649 Constellation, a new version involving a 50 per cent redesign and intended to take advantage of the extra power of the 'BD-1 engines to offer improved payload,

a faster cruising speed and greater economy, as well as improved passenger accommodation and a quieter cabin with better heating, cooling and ventilation. New propellers and an increase in flap deflection were also featured. The integral wing tankage was increased to 4,690 US gal and the maximum gross weight rose to 94,000lb, or 4,000lb more than that at which the 049 had been certificated; the landing weight was now 84,500olb. The Speedpak detachable ventral freight container was first used on the Model L-649 and the first—and as it turned out the only—customer for this particular version was Eastern Air Lines which ordered fourteen, plus a repeat order for seven placed later but delivered as L-749s, for its major routes, in particular the 'plum' New York–Miami holiday route. Eastern's first L-649 was delivered on 13 May 1947, Eastern having previously evaluated Model 049 NC70000. It is interesting to note that at this time Lockheed actually proposed the 2,400bhp (maximum take-off) Pratt & Whitney R-2800-CA15 or the 2,300bhp R-2800-CA17 Double Wasp as an alternative powerplant for Constellation customers, following tests of the re-engined prototype designated XC-69E. Most probably, the object was to win over from Douglas any airlines that preferred Pratt & Whitney to the still relatively untried Wright R-3350 but, in fact, no Constellations were built with the R-2800 engines.

The first of fourteen Model 649s for Eastern was delivered in May 1947 and all were converted to 749s in 1950; the 649 was the first model to use the Speedpak

The Model L-749

The increasing post-war interest shown by airlines in long-range transcontinental and overwater flights led to the rapid development of a long-range version of the L-649 and this, the Model L-749, soon outsold the former variant. It featured an additional 565 US gal fuel tank in each outer wing to bring the total tankage up to 5,820 US gal. This location of the extra tanks enabled the maximum gross weight to be increased to 102,000lb and the landing weight to 87,500lb without increasing the spar-bending moment at the wing root, because fuel distribution in the wing and the sequence of its usage by the engines was controlled. As a result, there was a small increase in payload, while the range was increased by 1,000 miles carrying the same payload as the 649. The Models 649 and 749 were produced in parallel, the first 749 being delivered to Air France on 18 April 1947, and these two new variants were originally known as Gold Plate Constellations, a name that was soon dropped, however.

Because the Model 049s had originally been laid down as C-69C and C-69D military transports, full advantage could not be taken of the possibilities offered by the structural design when installing seats, furnishings and air-conditioning, although standards of

KLM Model 049 PH-TEN Nijmegen *with Speedpak detached, showing its size and shape. KLM's last two 049s, PH-TEN and 'TEO, had a higher empty weight than the first four*

comfort were well up to what the airlines wanted. To reduce noise and vibration, the cabin walls of the 649 and 749 were mounted so that there was no 'solid' contact with the fuselage skin other than at the cabin windows. Several layers of fibreglass insulation and air spaces provided very effective damping, these layers and the inner layer of fire-resistant fabric being rubber-mounted from the skin. The broadcloth-covered and fully adjustable passenger seats were also designed to reduce vibration and were not flexibly mounted to remove the risk of adjacent seats jamming. The seats could be reclined, or the backs could be folded flat to form a lower berth 6ft 6in long from every two pairs of seats. The upper berths folded down from the walls, from above the windows, and rest bunks forward were provided for the crew for overwater routes although, on domestic routes when a navigator was not carried, the crew rest space was sacrificed in favour of more passenger seats.

Lockheed offered a choice of ten different cabin arrangements to Model 649 and 749 customers, seating from forty-four to sixty-four passengers, and six of these were sleeper layouts. In some layouts, every second pair of seats was reversible either for a party

travelling together, or for those who preferred to face aft. A typical seat pitch, in the overwater Model 649-79-34 46-passenger interior convertible to twenty-two sleeper berths plus two more in seats, was 41in between centres, with a seat width (excluding arms) of $18\frac{1}{2}$in and a central gangway width of 20in. On most cabin layouts seating was four-abreast, although a higher density layout, such as the 64-passenger '-12 interior, had five-abreast seating for the first seven rows and a correspondingly reduced seat pitch. The improved soundproofing of the 649 and 749 resulted in a cabin sound level of less than 93 decibels at frequencies of 75–150cps and less than 63 decibels from the frequency range 1,200–2,400cps when cruising at 20,000ft at 65 per cent METO power. An important consequence of the Reading accident which had resulted in the Constellation's grounding was the development of smoke evacuation procedures for all transport aircraft. The drill for the Constellation was now to remove one emergency exit over the wing and to keep the cockpit sliding windows and crew door closed, smoke from whatever cause then being sucked out and the flight deck kept clear of it. In addition, fireproofing standards were established for cabin interior materials and insulation and had to be complied with by all new commercial transports seeking certification by the CAA.

The Speedpak

Mention has already been made of the imaginatively-named Speedpak detachable under-fuselage freight container devised by Lockheed to augment the somewhat limited capacity (434cu ft) of the two underfloor freight holds. The Speedpak was first used on the Model 649, although it was also employed by several airlines, such as KLM and El Al, on their Model 049s, and it took advantage of the aircraft's 'lifting fuselage' with its cambered centreline and slightly drooped nose. The concept of a detachable external cargo container was not new; it had been applied during World War II to transport conversions of bombers such as the Vickers Warwick and Handley Page Halifax C.VIII.

The Constellation's Speedpak was evolved in its present form after extensive wind-tunnel tests of various external cargo panniers and its streamlined shape had no adverse effect on the handling characteristics and reduced the speed by only about 12mph. When first flight-tested on a C-69, it had a total volume of 400cu ft and measured 33ft long by 7ft wide by 3ft in depth, with an empty weight of 1,800lb. It could carry up to 8,200lb of freight and be fitted with special removable compartments which could be off-loaded or loaded at intermediate stops along a long-haul route; the Speedpak's maximum payload of four tons could be carried on stages of up to 1,000 miles. Loading and unloading was by means of a self-contained electric hoist in the Speedpak that lowered it to the ground; this could, it was claimed, be done in two minutes, thus shortening the ground time for handling cargo and baggage. Handling the Speedpak on the ground was facilitated by a pair of semi-recessed wheels mounted underneath at each end which enabled it to be moved away from beneath the aircraft. Yet although the Speedpak was well suited to freight shipments of high urgency and fairly small dimensions, its size, and particularly its depth, were such that it could not accommodate the larger loads that could be got through the freight doors of such types as the Douglas DC-4 and DC-6A. And, of course, an external container, however well streamlined, involved extra drag and consequent reduction in speed, unlike freight doors whose only penalty was the weight of the fuselage stiffening around the door cut-outs. Thus, the Constellation's true potentialities as a commercial freighter were not to be realised until the Model L-1049D Super Constellation, with forward and aft freight doors and developed from the US Navy's R7V-1, went into service in 1954. Meanwhile, in 1953, the exclusive world-wide manufacturing rights for the Speedpak had been sold to the French company SECAN (Société d'Etudes et de Constructions Aéronavales) of Gennevilliers.

To overcome the Speedpak's dimensional disadvantages—and also, perhaps, because by the late 1950s these containers were no longer so readily obtainable—several second-hand Model L-749As were, in fact, fitted with forward freight doors. One of these was LV-PBH, acquired by the Argentine charter operator Aerolineas Carreras TA on 10 July 1964; this

Royal Air Maroc 749A CN-CCP was one of several fitted with a forward freight door; the door hinge fairings can be seen just behind the star insignia on the nose

had been operated by Air-India International and later by Aeronaves de Mexico SA. It had undergone a major rebuild in which its rear fuselage (excluding the tail) had been removed and replaced by that of the US Navy's turboprop test-bed R7V-2 Super Constellation 131630 together with its rear freight doors, this resulting in a hybrid aircraft. Two of Royal Air Maroc's five Model L-749As acquired from Air France were also fitted with forward freight doors (one of them apparently retained its Speedpak as well) and one of these was sold to the Peruvian operator Copisa (Compania Peruana Internacional de Aviacion SA) in mid-1967. The British independent Aviation Charter Enterprises, or ACE Freighters as it was popularly known, acquired seven L-749As from 1964 onwards, four of them ex-South African Airways (two of these never had a British C of A issued) and the rest ex-BOAC aircraft which had been modified to incorporate a large rear freight door. Two of these were among a quartet acquired from BOAC by the British independent, Skyways, early in 1959 to replace Handley Page Hermes on the London-Singapore freight service then operated by Skyways under contract to BOAC. The Corporation converted all but one of them for Skyways to have a single upward-opening rear cargo door measuring 6ft high by 10ft wide, in which the passenger door was inset, and stronger freight floors. They were also used to operate the London-Tunis-Malta route for BEA with a 65-passenger cabin interior, and one was sold to the Austrian charter operator Aero Transport in the summer of 1963, and then to the Luxembourg charter company Interocean Airways SA a year later.

Further Weight Growth

With the Models 649 and 749 well established in airline service, Lockheed continued the pursuit of weight growth and increased allowable payload, and to this end proceeded to review the stress analyses, landing-gear service reports and drawings to evolve the next version. This was the Model L-749A in which, by means of comparatively small wing and undercarriage modifications, the maximum gross weight was increased to 107,000lb and the payload by 5,000lb, the maximum landing weight being 89,500lb and the zero fuel weight 87,500lb. This increase was achieved by fitting brakes of greater capacity, tyres of increased ply rating, stronger main landing gear axles and shock strut

cylinders; the wing centre-section and inner wing stubs were also reinforced and the centre fuselage strengthened. The Model L-749A was revealed in the spring of 1949; the first new Constellation operators to order this variant were South African Airways, which bought four, but by the time these were delivered in 1950 many existing L-749s had been converted to L-749A standard, and during 1949 alone Lockheed issued ninety-eight special kits to operators for modifying their Constellations up to L-749A standard to take advantage of the higher payload.

A similar modification was proposed for the 649 which, by further strengthening of the inner wing and stronger main landing gear shock struts, became the Model L-649A with a maximum gross weight of 98,000lb and a landing weight of 89,500lb, the fuel tankage remaining the same. This variant was overtaken in the project stage by Eastern's conversion of all but one of its first 14 L-649s (which had been lost in an accident) to L-749s in 1950 with the extra outer wing tanks of this model and higher gross weight, the remaining seven aircraft of the repeat order being delivered as Model L-749s. And not long before the L-749A was revealed, Lockheed announced, in June 1948, that Model 749s due for delivery from the spring of 1949 could be modified to increase the maximum gross weight to 105,000lb and the landing weight to 87,500lb by a few comparatively minor structural modifications to the inner wings and main landing gear. Most operators, however, preferred to take advantage of the Model L-749A on which the Speedpak could now be carried at any load factors up to stage lengths of 2,200 miles. Take-off and climb performance at the higher 749A gross weight was not only maintained but actually improved by the use of Curtiss Electric 830 airscrews instead of the Curtiss Electric 850s previously fitted, the former resulting in a take-off run of 2,160ft and the latter 2,450ft at 107,000lb.

Continuing the theme of product improvement, an aluminium plastic Plycor flooring was developed in 1949 for the 749A and 749 which resulted in a weight saving of 194lb over the previous type of floor, and a fireproof coating for the engine oil tanks was also made available, as well as improved brakes and undercarriage hydraulic damping. A new type of NACA air scoop under the upper half of each cowling was developed, tipped down so as to exclude dust and rain and the last few Model L-749As to be built were fitted with 'jet stacks'—a form of exhaust thrust augmentation that reduced back pressure in the exhaust system and added, it was claimed, as much as 15mph to the maximum cruising speed, but at the expense of an abrupt increase in cabin noise level. 'Jet stacks' could be fitted retrospectively to 749s already built. Performance could also be improved by the fitting of Curtiss Electric Model C6345 three-blade reversible-pitch airscrews which featured automatic synchronisation for the maintenance of uniform engine speeds working independently of the engines' oil supplies, a refinement that made for a quieter cabin as well as improved take-off and climb performance.

Following the crash near Chicago of TWA Model 049 N86511 *Star of Paris* on 1 September 1961 with the loss of all seventy-three passengers and five crew aboard (this aircraft had inaugurated TWA's North Atlantic services fifteen years earlier) modifications were made to the elevator boost shifting system on all Constellations and Super Constellations in US airline, Air Force and Navy service. It was found that this accident had been caused by the shedding of a bolt from the parallelogram linkage of the elevator boost mechanism, apparently through improper assembly. The bolt was probably shed during initial climb-out and its loss would have caused the boost to apply up elevator and the pilot(s) to push hard on the control column(s) to stop the nose rising sharply. This, in turn, would have reduced, or excluded, any possibility of moving the shift handle of the elevator boost system and, as subsequent tests showed, the likely result was that that part of the tailplane to which the starboard fin was attached separated from the aircraft before it crashed. Following a few previous accidents with US Navy and Air Force Super Constellations, the CAB had already recommended a modification to enable the elevator boost shifting system to be operated without restriction, regardless of pilot-applied control forces.

Another cause of several previous accidents had been the inability to feather an overspeeding propeller, and this led to the loss of a Linea Aeropostal Venezolana Model L-1049E Super Constellation on 20 June 1956 on a flight from New York to Caracas. Overspeeding of No 2 propeller had been reported by the pilot, Capt Luis Plata, who was unable to feather it; he turned back for New York but when fifty miles away received permission to start dumping fuel. Shortly afterwards, the aircraft exploded and dived into the sea, killing all the sixty-four passengers and ten crew, and it was believed that the overspeeding prop had come off while fuel was being dumped and that the fuel had ignited. A lawsuit resulted from this accident and in 1963 damages of $387,387 were awarded to the wife and daughter of one of the victims by a US Federal Judge, who also held United Aircraft Corporation's Hamilton Standard Division negligent in failing to provide a pitch lock which would probably have prevented the accident.

An Early Airline Radar

An interesting modification test-flown in a TWA Constellation in the summer of 1947 was what might well have been the world's first production collision-warning radar—nearly a decade before airborne radar came into general use in airliners. This was demonstrated in a Constellation by Howard Hughes, whose Hughes Aircraft Co's electronics division had de-

The first Model 749 to be built was XA-GOQ for Aerovias Guest SA of Mexico, which sold it to Air France in January 1949 as F-BAZR. It was later used by Turboméca as an engine test-bed

veloped and manufactured it after extensive tests. Flight trials followed in a Douglas C-47 used by TWA for research, the airline's pilots and engineers were very favourably impressed, and there were high hopes that TWA would instal it in all of its 114-aircraft fleet within four or five weeks. Hughes actually announced that it would be made available to other airlines at cost price, estimated at only about $135 (£34), a far cry from the very sophisticated and costly anti-collision radars (around $30,000 each) that were being talked about in the late 1960s when air traffic congestion and near misses had become a major problem.

Such cheapness naturally implied a very basic and simple form of radar, the Hughes set, which weighed only 16lb, being a combined transmitter and receiver operating on frequencies of 420 to 450 megacycles. Two small antennae on either side of the nose sent out pulses at the rate of 40 per second in a cone of nearly 180 degrees included angle in front of the aircraft. The reflection from any object, such as another aircraft, operated warning lights and a bell in the cockpit but did not indicate its direction or height relative to the receiver. The radar could be set to give warnings at various distances, the two settings used on the demonstration model being 2,000ft and 500ft, the latter being intended primarily for instrument landings. Although very primitive by comparison with the airborne radars of the mid-1950s, and lacking pictorial presentation of a converging aircraft's path, this Hughes radar of 1947 might well have been developed into something rather more sophisticated which would have met the already evident problem of near misses. Perhaps the real reason why nothing more was heard of it was that this problem was still thought to be solvable by the 'see and be seen' philosophy.

Yet there had already been several cases of transport aircraft colliding with other aircraft—sometimes escaping with serious damage—and there were many more instances on record of airliners flying into high ground or mountains. The former happened to Pan American Model L-749 N86530 *Clipper Monarch of the Skies* on 30 January 1949 a few minutes after it had taken off from New York's La Guardia airport on a London flight. At about 4,000ft, a single-engined Cessna 170 with a pilot and passenger collided with the Constellation, ripping a 15ft hole in the forward part of the upper fuselage, in which the Cessna's engine remained jammed. The two occupants of the Cessna

were killed, but miraculously none of the twenty-nine people aboard the Constellation was injured. The captain and co-pilot, with a fine display of airmanship, made a safe landing at the USAF base at Mitchell Field in New York State, and, despite the huge hole and some skin buckling, the forward fuselage successfully withstood the strain of the landing.

New Constellation Operators

Pan American's *Clipper Monarch of the Skies* was one of four sold to Air France in December 1949 to replace the 049s the French airline had sold to TWA. And while Lockheed was evolving the weight increases and other improvements to the Models 649, 749 and 749A, the last two versions were going into service not only with satisfied 049 customers like Pan American, Air France, KLM, TWA and BOAC but also with several operators newly established on the international scene. Among the latter were Qantas and Air-India, for which the Connie was to be the means of establishing a fine reputation in the big league of international air transport. But this ambition was not always fulfilled, as in the case of the Mexican airline Aerovias Guest SA, which had been founded in 1946 by an American, Winston Guest, in conjunction with Mexican interests. The company had started a Mexico City-Madrid DC-4 service, with stops at Miami (no traffic rights were held here until 1950), Bermuda, the Azores and Lisbon, on 8 January 1948 and three Model L-749s ordered for this new route were allotted the registrations XA-GOQ, XA-GOR and XA-GOS. The first of these was, in fact, the first Model L-749 to be built, going into service with Guest in July 1948 and visiting London Airport on the 8th of that month bringing Mexican competitors to the Olympic Games. But the Madrid route did not prove to be a success and, after the frequency had been reduced in the summer of 1951, was suspended completely by the end of that year. Guest was unable to obtain traffic rights to New York because of a long disagreement between Mexico and the USA over a bilateral air agreement, unresolved until 1957 when another Mexican airline, Aeronaves de Mexico, was given New York rights. This meant that Guest was unable to take delivery of its second and third L-749s, and XA-GOQ was sold after only four months service on the Mexico City-Miami route through Lockheed to Air France, with whom it became F-BAZR.

Miami for a time was the only point in the States to which Guest had traffic rights, and to get round this obstacle a route to Windsor, Ontario—the Canadian city just across the border from Detroit—was opened in 1955 with two Model L-749As acquired from Qantas in October and November of that year. The Windsor route proved to be uneconomic and was discontinued in October 1957, the airline continuing Constellation services to Panama and later to Caracas.

Another Constellation operation destined to be short-lived was that of the Irish airline, Aerlinte Eireann, formed in 1947 to operate Atlantic services from Shannon and co-owned with the major Irish operator of European routes, Aer Lingus Teoranta. Five L-749s were ordered for a service to New York, the first of these being delivered on 26 August 1947,

Aerlinte Eireann took delivery of five 749s in 1947 to operate services to New York but sold them to BOAC shortly after; EI-ACS St Patrick *seen here became G-ALAL* Banbury

but following a change of government policy, the New York service planned for 1948 (thrice-weekly flights to Boston and New York were to have started on St Patrick's Day—17 March) was shelved and the Constellations were put on to the Aer Lingus Dublin-London route for a time, from 3 November 1947. But

Originally delivered to Howard Hughes in June 1951 as N6025C, and named Star of Colorado *for TWA but never operated by them, 749A G-ANNT* Buckingham *was bought by BOAC in 1954*

ZS-DBR Cape Town, delivered in April 1950, was South African Airways' first 749A

they were really too big for Aer Lingus routes at this stage, and the following summer all five were sold for £315,000 each (£65,000 more than the Irish airline had paid per aircraft) to BOAC, who found themselves in the happy position of getting these, their first L-749s, without any dollar expenditure; they were later modified to 749A standard.

The government of Ceylon also ordered two Constellations in 1947 for the international routes of the newly-formed Ceylon Airways, which soon became Air Ceylon. But this order later lapsed, as Australian National Airways operated two DC-4s under contract for Air Ceylon's Colombo-London service from February 1949, and later from Colombo to Darwin and Sydney. These services ceased in October 1953 and it was not until February 1956 that KLM started a weekly 'Sapphire' service to Amsterdam and London for Air Ceylon with a Model L-749A, replacing this with an L-1049E Super Constellation in November 1958. The 749A was fitted with twelve 'SleepAir' reclining sleeper-seats and seats for up to thirty-five more tourist passengers.

Perhaps for no other operator did the Constellation and Super Constellation do as much in establishing a reputation as Air–India International—aided very considerably by the airline's reputation for superlative

Ex-Eastern 649 N103A seen here was operated by Associated Air Transport Inc, one of the smaller US 'non-skeds'

cabin service epitomised in its advertising by the smiling figure of 'The Maharajah'. Three L-749s were ordered and on 8 June 1948 one of these began the first Bombay-London service via Cairo and Geneva. Initially, the service was once-weekly but more flights were soon scheduled with alternative intermediate stops, and Delhi and Calcutta were added to the international network. A Bombay-Nairobi service was also started on 21 January 1950 via Karachi and Aden, not long after delivery of a pair of new 749As, followed by two more a year later. Following delivery of the final pair, Air–India sold two of its earlier model 749s to Qantas.

One of the last two 749As acquired by Air–India, VT-DEP *Kashmir Princess*, was the victim of sabotage; it crashed on 11 April 1955 off Sarawak with the loss of fifteen lives while on a flight between Hong Kong and Djakarta carrying a party of Chinese Communist officials and journalists to the Afro-Asian conference at Bandoeng. The culprit was found to be Chow Tseming, alias Chou, an airport cleaner employed by the Hong Kong Aircraft Engineering Corporation, who had planted a small time bomb in the 749 in return for a payment, alleged to have been £37,500, made by persons connected with a Kuomintang (Chinese Nationalist) intelligence organisation. Air–India's remaining three 749s were traded in to Lockheed in 1958 for resale to Aeronaves de Mexico after being replaced by Super Constellations. Other Latin American 749 operators were Linea Aeropostal Venezolana, with two, and Avianca of Colombia, which took delivery of two 749As in May 1951 before introducing Super Constellations later, and acquiring three more ex-BOAC and one ex-TWA 749As in 1959.

Qantas Empire Airways really began to make its mark internationally with the 749, four of which were delivered in October 1947 and went into service on the 'Kangaroo' route from Sydney to London on 1 December. This was the first Qantas service right through to London, previous services having been joint BOAC/Qantas ones with 'Hythe'-class Sunderland flying boats, Qantas crews taking over at Karachi for Sydney. Two more 749s were bought from Air–India, and frequencies of London flights were stepped up to four a week, with new stopping-places. On 1 September 1952 a 749 inaugurated the 'Wallaby' route across the Indian Ocean from Sydney, Melbourne and Perth to Johannesburg, via the Cocos Islands and

Mauritius, at a once-fortnightly frequency, later alternating with a South African Airways flight over the same route with 749As to provide a weekly service. Qantas sold four of its 749s to BOAC in 1954 and 1955 and the remaining two to Guest of Mexico for a total of some £4,300,000 with spares, a price not far from their original first cost in 1947. Qantas 749s originally seated thirty-eight daytime passengers (and later sixty) with provision for berths, but in June 1950 sleeping berths were removed in favour of baggage racks, as they were from BOAC's 749s on the Australia route, and the berth windows were then removed.

South African Airways' first 749A was delivered on 24 April 1950 and the airline began Constellation services to London on 26 August of that year, and from November 1957 across the Indian Ocean to Perth. To meet BOAC's Comet competition, SAA leased two Comet 1s from the Corporation for its 'Springbok' services to London, converting the 749As for tourist-class services. After the 1954 accidents grounded the Comet, the 749As resumed first-class services, and two years later were put on the more important domestic routes, like Johannesburg-Durban. Replaced by DC-7Bs, they were put up for sale and cocooned in 1959 but two returned to service the following year for low-fare domestic flights and two more were leased to the South African independent, Trek Airways, in 1961. Trek specialised in low-fare, low-frequency flights to Europe. All four were finally sold to ACE Freighters in 1964.

In the US domestic field, the only new 749 operator was Chicago & Southern Airlines, which took delivery of the first of six Model 749-79-60 Constellations on 1 August 1950 mainly for its routes from Chicago and other mid-West cities, Houston and New Orleans to Havana, Kingston (Jamaica), San Juan (Puerto Rico) and Caracas (Venezuela); these C & S aircraft were later modified to 749A standard with 'jet stacks' and had accommodation for fifty-seven passengers. Chicago & Southern merged with Delta Airlines of Atlanta on 1 May 1953 and, as a result, three of its 749As were sold to TWA in April and June 1954 and three others to Pacific Northern Airlines, which operated them from Seattle to points in Alaska. Delta itself later acquired four 049s from Pan American, in February 1956. Capital Airlines purchased seven ex-KLM Model 749A-79-24s which had been traded in to Lockheed's from the late summer of 1951 against the Super

VH-EAB Lawrence Hargrave, *named after an early Australian pioneer of powered flight, was one of the first four Qantas 749s*

Constellations the Dutch airline had ordered. Capital placed a contract with KLM at the end of 1951 for the modification and refurbishing of these Constellations to its own requirements, which included the installation of completely new cabin interiors and certain technical modifications to equip the aircraft for US domestic services. All but two of the seven were ferried out from KLM's Schiphol workshops to the States in 1953 but after barely two years' service with Capital they were ferried back across the Atlantic to Britain for refurbishing to BOAC's standards as part of the exchange of 049s and 749As negotiated between the two airlines following the 1954 Comet accidents. At about the same time the Corporation also acquired four 749s from Qantas and one from Howard Hughes, originally destined for TWA, bringing the total of 749s operated by BOAC up to seventeen. In 1955 these seated sixty passengers in the all-tourist configuration in five-abreast rows of Vickers reclining seats. Two additional cargo compartments could be arranged at the front of the cabin after the removal of six seats on the starboard side.

KLM put into service a total of twenty Model 749-79-33s and 749-79-24s (modified up to 749A

Trans-California Airlines operated 98-passenger 649s, including N105A (seen here), on low-fare services within California

standard) the first of which, PH-TEP *Pontianak*, was delivered on 13 August 1947. These were used primarily on the transatlantic routes to New York, Montreal and Curacao and on the service to Djakarta in Indonesia. Their original cabin layout was for forty-six passengers but later an all-sleeper interior with thirty berths was adopted for the 'Cosmopolitan' sleeper service from Amsterdam to New York, while in 1951 a 61-passenger interior was featured on a number of flights carrying Dutch emigrants to Australia.

Air France's 749 and 749A fleet, twenty-four in all, went into service during 1947–51 on routes to Canada and the USA, to the French Caribbean islands such as Guadeloupe and Martinique, to South America, the Far East and Africa, particularly to French West and Equatorial Africa. The fleet included four Model 749-79-46s acquired from Pan American in December 1949; these were Pan Am's only 749s, the airline having gone over to the Boeing Stratocruiser for its first-line equipment of the 1950s. Air France featured a very spacious de-luxe interior for 'The Parisian' service to New York, seating only sixteen passengers in the 749's cabin (replacing a previous 24-berth sleeper interior), and giving them the sort of leg-room to be found only in executive aircraft. Three 749s were leased to Air Inter for the latter's domestic routes during April–September 1961 and a few L-1049Gs the following year. And Air Vietnam leased 749s from Air France from 1957 for its Saigon–Hong Kong route, these being replaced by L-1049s.

TWA was the largest 749 operator with twelve Model L-749s and twenty-five Model L-749As supplementing the 049s both on US domestic and the international route through Paris, Rome and the Near East to Bombay. Following the inauguration of Atlantic services in February 1946, TWA's routes were extended eastwards to India, reaching Bombay on 5 January 1947. The original plan had been to continue on to Shanghai, in China, linking up there with Northwest Orient Airlines (which had rights to serve a number of cities in China from the USA) to establish a joint round-the-world service. The CAB had awarded TWA a seven-year certificate for the USA–China route on 5 July 1945 and the Bombay–Shanghai portion would have been via Calcutta, Mandalay, Hanoi (then capital of French Indo-China) and Canton. But the establishment of a Communist regime in place of Chiang Kai-shek and the proclamation of the Chinese People's Republic in September 1949 closed that country to Western airlines, and without through traffic to China services beyond Bombay could not be justified. Although politics at that time thwarted full achievement of the ambition reflected in the airline's title of Trans World Airlines (used as a promotional name from 1946, but in 1950 voted by stockholders as the new name to replace Transcontinental & Western Air Inc), TWA was the most important international as well as domestic Constellation operator. A variety of interiors was featured in its 749 fleet, including a 32-seater 'Sleeper Seat' layout with reclining seats, a 60-seat tourist interior for the Atlantic, an 81-seat layout for US domestic coach routes and a de-luxe 18-berth sleeper layout for 'The London Ambassador' service to London, started on 8 April 1951. Altogether 131 Model 749s and 749As were built, including two PO-1Ws and ten C-121 military versions.

4: New Versions: New Operators

As the post-war world's diplomacy and politics became increasingly set in the Cold War mould the Constellation went back into uniform again in two new military versions: the C-121A personnel and staff transport (plus the VC-121B variant for VIPs) and the PO-1W for the AEW (Airborne Early Warning) role. This latter was to become the most important military task of the Lockheed transport, eventually involving the RC-121 and WV-2 Super Constellation variants in around-the-clock surveillance of the North American coastlines and ocean approaches. The PO-1W was developed by Lockheed from the 749A for the US Navy Bureau of Aeronautics as a flying radar station able to operate at high altitudes and thus overcome the limitations imposed by a curving horizon on the straight line transmission of unbending radar beams. The two PO-1Ws built, nicknamed 'Po' Ones', proved the basic feasibility of the AEW idea, which enabled detection of surface ships, submarines or aircraft to be extended far beyond anything previously possible. As well as providing a potent tool for detection and long-range sea search, this concept could also be applied to the direction of bomber interceptions by friendly fighters. For these tasks, great range and endurance were essential and this was achieved in the Super Constellation AEW variants by adding 2,200 US gal extra tankage over that of the airline Model L-1049.

The AEW Constellations were easily distinguished by a very large 'top hat'-like dorsal radome amidships containing Airborne Early Warning radar, and a smaller ventral radome under the fuselage. On the Super Constellation the latter measured approximately 19ft × 29ft and was elliptical in plan view, but on the PO-1W the ventral radome was smaller; the dorsal radome was about 8ft high. Weather radar was also installed in the nose, and the PO-1W featured eight small stub-like aerials along the top of the fuselage and two more protruding from the starboard side of the lower rear fuselage. A crew of twenty-two could be carried, made up largely of radar operators and technicians, and for long flights bunks were provided for relief crews. Instead of passenger seats, the cabin interior was taken up by radar monitoring stations and the associated 'black boxes', while galley facilities and rest bunks provided a degree of crew comfort far above that of World War II patrol bombers. The spaciousness of a pressurised and soundproofed airliner interior was not just an incidental luxury for the AEW role; it enhanced operational efficiency by reducing crew fatigue and diminishing noise, and it also left plenty of space for the advanced radar systems,

The two PO-1Ws were used to test the basic feasibility of the airborne early warning concept, and had a smaller ventral radome than the WV-2/EC-121 versions

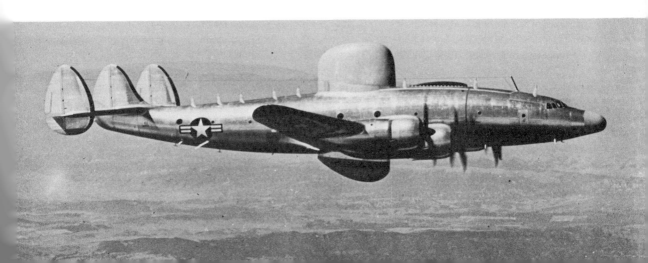

The first WV-1, BuAer 124437, was used by the FAA as N119 for navaid calibration with the radomes removed, a rear cargo door and normal 749-type cabin windows

which could be progressively updated with the minimum disturbance to the aircraft proper as new advances in electronics were made or new counter-measures developed by the other side.

The first PO-1W, serialled 124437, made its maiden flight on 9 June 1949 and was handed over to the US Navy on 5 April 1950. It was later coded XD-9 and named *Woden*, and went into service with VX-4 special duties squadron like its sister PO-1W, serialled 124438, which was delivered on 12 August 1949. Flight testing proved the Constellation to be a stable platform for the early warning role in spite of the substantial size of the two radomes. A small increase in tail unit area was later found necessary on the PO-1Ws to counter-act the additional side area of the radomes, the outer vertical surfaces being increased to L-1049 size, but the triple fins and rudders were particularly well adapted to these extra protuberances because the air-flow around the outer fins was not disturbed in any way by flow disturbances around the fuselage. The PO-1W (the suffix 'W' in this designation denoting 'special search') was redesignated WV-1 early in 1952, and the power plants were four 2,500bhp (maximum take-off) Wright R-3350-75s.

The WV-1s served the US Navy for several more years while the WV-2 and RC-121 Super Constellation AEW variants were going into production and squadron service, but in 1958 both WV-1s were disposed of to the Federal Aviation Agency, where they

joined three other 749s, two ex-TWA and one ex-Eastern, used by the FAA for flight-checking and calibrating navaids in the Pacific. The first WV-1, BuAer 124437, was registered N119 and 124438 became N120. Both were out of service by early 1965, the former being subsequently registered N1192 and going into storage with the USAF; in 1968 it was re-registered to the FAA. The other WV-1 was re-registered N1206 for disposal, and later went to the Schilling Institute of Kansas, which passed it on to Kansas Surplus Property.

For the navaid calibration role, the WV-1s had their dorsal and ventral radomes removed and in place of the AEW interior the cabin was converted to a mixed cargo/passenger arrangement with a flight inspection console forward, a stronger freight floor with tied-down points being featured, as well as a rear cargo door. The ex-TWA and Eastern 749s had interiors very similar to those of their airline days, apart from the addition of a flight inspection console on the starboard side aft of the flight engineer's panel. Two of them were also fitted with Speedpaks. A typical crew complement for a calibration mission consisted of two pilots, an engineer, a navigator, a flight inspection technician (at the console) and a cabin attendant, while a wide range of radio receivers and transceivers, such as dual VOR/ILS, was installed.

The former Eastern 749 N116 (ex-N116A), crashed at Topham Field, Canton Island on 26 April 1962 with the loss of four crew members and one passenger. Canton Island had been a stopping point on Pan American's flying-boat services through Hawaii to New Zealand before Pearl Harbour, but was no longer used by regular airline services. Another FAA 749, N65 (ex-TWA's N6012C *Star of Massachusetts*) was lost in an accident on 15 August 1966.

The Lockheed C-121

Meanwhile, ten examples of the other new post-war military version of the Constellation, the C-121, had been ordered by the US Air Force for operation by the Military Air Transport Service, and whereas the original C-69 had been a military version of the Model 049, the C-121 was a version of the Model 749. It had a maximum gross weight of 102,000lb, and was stressed for cargo carrying with heavy freight flooring, and an upward-opening freight door aft. The engines were four 2,500bhp Wright R-3350-75s. Seats could be removed to accommodate stretchers in a casualty evacuation role and C-121s also played a part in the Berlin airlift, which began in May 1948. Seven of them flew 5·9 million passenger-miles in their first month in service carrying personnel and supplies from Westover Air Force Base, Massachusetts, to Frankfurt's Rhein-Main airport. Thereafter the C-121s were used mainly as staff and VIP transports.

The ten C-121s ordered by the USAF were serialled 48-608 to 48-617 and were made up of eight C-121A-1-LO personnel and staff transports, one VC-121A-1-LO and one VC-121B-1-LO, the latter being a luxury VVIP and staff transport for the use of commanders-in-chief. The first VC-121B to be built as such, 48-608, was also the first of the C-121s and was delivered to the USAF on 12 November 1948, while six of the C-121As, which as delivered had air-liner-type seating for between forty-four and sixty-four passengers, were later modified up to VC-121B standard after a few years in service.

General Dwight D. Eisenhower used VC-121A-1-LO 48-610, named *Columbine II* after the state flower of Colorado, his wife's native state, when he was com-

mander of SHAPE (Supreme Headquarters Allied Powers Europe) from December 1950 to June 1952. *Columbine II* was later used by General Alfred M. Gruenther when he took over command of SHAPE from General Ridgeway in 1953, and weather radar was fitted in the nose at a later date. Generals Eisenhower and Gruenther also both used C-121A-1-LO 48-614, while the former *Columbine II* was registered N9970E late in 1955 to the US Department of National Defence and was operated under contract for a short time by Pan American as *Clipper Fortuna*. It later reverted to its military serial and became a VC-121B. Another C-121A also obtained a civil identity when 48-616 was acquired by TWA in 1957 for lease to Ethiopian Airlines (with whom TWA had had a management contract since 1945) both for airline use and as a personal transport for the Emperor Hailé Selassie. Re-registered ET-T-35, this C-121A was delivered to Ethiopia on 2 June 1957, complete with a state-room for the Emperor which could be removed when the aircraft was used for normal airline services. Less than six weeks after delivery, on 10 July, it force-landed fifty miles north of Khartoum with two engines on fire, and although there were no casualties the aircraft was a total loss.

Of the other C-121A-1-LOs, General Douglas MacArthur used 48-613 during the Korean campaign, when it was named *Bataan*, General Hoyt S. Vandenburg, Chief of Staff of the USAF, used 48-615, named *Dewdrop*, while another, unnamed, was used by General George Marshall. MacArthur's *Bataan* was eventually acquired as a transport by the National Aeronautics and Space Administration for use by the Goddard Space Flight Centre at Greenbelt, Maryland,

C-121A-1-LO 48-614 Columbine *was used by General Eisenhower and later by General Gruenther as a VIP transport*

C-121A 48-616 was leased to Ethiopian Airlines as ET-T-35 for the use of both the airline and the Emperor Hailé Selassie. Note the Lion of Judah insignia in gold on the fuselage

who operated it with the serial number NASA 422, later registered N422NA, while 48-612 was in use by the US Army in 1967. C-121A 48-611 was named *United States of America*, and the rather piquant situation arose in the early 1950s of the US Commanders-in-Chief having at their disposal in the C-121s a larger and slightly faster VIP transport than President Truman himself, who was then using a Douglas DC-6 named *The Independence*. When Eisenhower succeeded Truman, a C-121A became the Presidential aircraft in early 1953 and was replaced in August 1954 by a VC-121E Super Constellation named *Columbine III*. The VIP C-121s were operated by the USAF's Special Air Missions squadron. By 1969, the surviving eight C-121A/VC-121B Constellations were all in storage and, later, five were sold to Christler Flying Service.

The Turboprop Challenge

While several types of US turboprop engines had been designed and run before 1950, some of them very powerful, most did not get beyond the experimental

stage and US airline interest in this type of power-plant in the early 1950s could best be described as largely academic. The Wright company had produced the XT35 turboprop of over 5,000hp and flown it in the nose of a Boeing B-17 in September 1947, but abandoned the project when a USAAF contract for the engine was cancelled. They then turned to a civil development of the R-3350 Turbo-Cyclone, or Turbo-Compound as it was later to become known. This had gone into production for several US Navy aircraft, including the Lockheed P2V-4 Neptune patrol bomber, and derived its name from the three 'blown-down' turbines connected to the exhaust ports and in turn directly geared through three fluid couplings to the engine crankshaft, thus converting into useful power about 20 per cent of the available heat energy normally lost through the exhaust gases. The three turbines were equally disposed around the engine on an extension of the rear cover, each being fed by short pipes from six cylinder exhaust ports. Although hardly venturesome in terms of new technology, and subject to some troubles in airline service, the Turbo-Compound was to power both the US contenders in the long-haul transport field, the Super Constellation and the Douglas DC-7, throughout the 1950s. It proved well able to meet the challenge posed by Britain's long-haul turboprop Britannia and Turbo-Compounds powered the first non-stop North Atlantic and US transcontinental services.

The Turbo-Compound's installation in the Model L-1049C Super Constellation, preceded by the Model L-1049A with a more powerful version of the conventional R-3350, led to proposed versions of the Model 749 with these newer powerplants. The first of these, the Model L-749B, was to have been powered by four of the 2,700bhp (maximum take-off) Wright R-3350-836C18CA-1 powerplants intended for the Model L-1049A, and was stressed for the future installation of turboprops; had airline interest demanded it, these engines could have been installed retrospectively in existing 749A and 749 airframes. The second design study was the Model L-849 Constellation, a proposed development of the 749 fitted with four R-3350 Turbo-Compounds similar to those of the Model L-1049C. This version had an all-up weight of 110,000lb and a maximum still air range of 5,600 miles with the same fuel tankage (5,820 US gal) of the 749 and 749A. Both the 749B and 849 were overtaken by the Super Constellation proper, as airlines preferred the additional fuselage stretch it offered in addition to the increased power which would not alone have made the 749B and 849 economic propositions.

In Britain, D. Napier and Son Ltd were the pioneers of turboprop re-engining and in 1955–56 had converted a Convair 340 first to two 3,200ehp NEl.1 Eland turboprops and later to 3,500ehp NEl.6 Elands; a Convair 440 was similarly converted in the States. Airline interest in the Eland for re-engining larger types such as the Constellation quickly grew, Lockheed studied it for use in the Electra and in the late summer of 1957 Panair do Brasil announced their intention of re-engining some of their Model 049 Constellations—eleven was the number reported at the time—with Napier Elands. Napiers estimated that an Eland-powered Model 749 would have a block speed about 50mph faster than the piston-engined type and that though maximum range with full payload would have been slightly reduced—since no increase in the 749's gross weight would have been practicable—the 749's aircraft-mile cost would be reduced by about 9d (4p) over stage lengths of from 300 to 2,000 miles.

In the event, however, the Eland-powered Constellation remained a project. Panair do Brasil's 049s were displaced as first-line equipment by DC-7Cs; in July 1961 Napiers were merged with Rolls-Royce, and the Eland was discontinued not long after. Four years later, in 1965, Panair do Brasil was declared bankrupt with debts totalling $62 million. Nine of its 049s had been in storage from 1962–63, one of these had been partly cannibalised and two had been damaged and left unrepaired. These lingered on (except for one) until four years after the airline's collapse, when, in April 1969, six were sold to a firm called Engenav and broken up at Rio's Galeao airport, while a seventh, PP-PDG, was painted in the livery of ASL Arruda Industria e Comercio, though it was not, apparently, ever flown by them. In 1972 it was bought by a Sao Paulo company called Empresa Amazonense Importaçao e Exportaçao but crashed on 29 May 1972.

The French Air Force operates a number of ex-Air France 749As modified for air-sea rescue work; note the observation blisters fore and aft

A new quasi-military variant of the Constellation appeared when the SGACC (Secretariat General à l'Aviation Civile et Commerciale), the French Government department in charge of civil aviation, acquired six Model L-749As from Air France in 1960 and had them extensively modified for air-sea rescue duties; two more ex-Air France 749As were acquired in 1964–5 and a third later. Externally the only differences shown by this variant were the four observation blisters, two on each side of the fuselage just behind the crew compartment and two aft just behind the rear entrance door, and some external aerials. No weather or search radar was fitted, but Bendix Doppler and other radio aids facilitated extended searches for crashed aircraft over sea or land, and the aircraft were equipped to drop survival kit containers from the open passenger door using an inclined ramp with rollers. They were operated by the SGACC's SAR section (the letters 'SAR' stand for Search and Rescue or, in French, Section Aérienne de Recherches) but later came under the control of the French Air Force's Commandement du Transport Aérien Militaire (CoTAM) and were operated by the Escadron Aérien de Recherche et Sauvetage 99 rescue unit, based at Toulouse-Francazals. They retained their civil registrations,

World Wide Airlines, whose 749A N4902C is seen here, was refused interim operating authority by the CAB in 1962

having special category certificates of airworthiness in the aerial work class, although under Air Force control.

New Operators

Like the Model 049s, the 649s and 749s sold off by the major airlines found a ready market among the smaller non-scheduled carriers, particularly the US 'non-skeds' and European charter operators. Smaller airlines elsewhere, particularly in Latin America, also found them attractive. Eastern Air Lines sold its remaining twelve Model 649s and five 749s to the Transit Equipment Co of New York late in 1960 for delivery before 1 January 1961, and Transit later sold them to California Airmotive. Before the sale, Eastern had occasionally leased at least one Constellation to Colonial Airlines which, although dating back to 1928 and with valuable routes from New York to Montreal and Bermuda, had remained a small airline. Both Eastern and National had tried at various times to take it over, and Eastern finally succeeded in doing so on 1 June 1956, thus acquiring the valuable route to Bermuda. A few of the ex-Eastern 649s and 749s were cannibalised for spares or stored and the nose section of one, N110A, was being used as a storehouse for garden tools near Idlewild Airport (later Kennedy International) towards the end of 1961.

Other 649s and 749s were disposed of, usually on lease from California Airmotive, to several of the smaller non-scheduled US carriers such as Standard

A Model 749A in the livery of a Peruvian operator, Trans-Peruana

Airways, Associated Air Transport, Modern Air Transport, California Hawaiian Airlines, Paramount Airlines, Pacific Air Transport, Great Lakes Airlines, Trans-California Airlines and Quaker City Airways (trading as Admiral Airways). Operators like Standard, Associated, Paramount and Quaker City leased their ex-Eastern 649s and 749s out to the other US 'nonskeds' as required. Standard sold N120A on 6 June 1963 to an unusual owner, Casino Operations, which was apparently an associate of Las Vegas Hacienda (the Hacienda Hotel) that operated several ex-TWA 049s and later itself owned N120A, before it passed on to several more owners. It eventually crashed on a farm near Aracatuba, Sao Paulo province, Brazil, on 4 August 1969 while on a smuggling flight. Trans-California Airlines used six leased 98-passenger Model 649s and 749s on scheduled low-fare Burbank-Oakland (San Francisco) intra-state services from 1962 but despite a very high passenger seating density—or perhaps because of it—this service could not compete with the Lockheed Electra turboprops of Pacific Southwest Airlines, the major California intra-state operator, and was soon discontinued.

One ex-Eastern 749, N118A, was acquired from California Airmotive by Air Haiti International SA, formed in March 1961 to operate as the designated Haitian flag airline from that country to Miami, New York, San Juan (Puerto Rico) and beyond to points in the British West Indies. Haiti's other airline, Compagnie Haitienne de Transports Aériens (COHATA), was a military airline that flew a domestic network only, and the country had previously relied solely on foreign airlines like Pan American for its international air links. Air Haiti's 749 was given the Haitian civil registration HH-ABA but the actual owners were the Airline Management & Investment Co, indicative of the foreign interests behind Air Haiti, which later applied, without success, to the CAB for a foreign air carrier permit to operate into the States. The airline's Constellation was lost at sea on 11 November 1961 on a flight from San Juan to Managua (Nicaragua), possibly through sabotage, and Air Haiti ceased operations.

The Constellation was pressed into a military role by one of the several Haitian emigré rebel groups in the States opposed to the oppressive regime of the President, the late 'Papa Doc' Duvalier. From time to time these groups have organised 'do it yourself' bombing raids over the capital, Port-au-Prince, usually with any surplus transport they could obtain and without much pretence at accuracy. One of these raids took place on 4 June 1969, when an ex-Pacific Northern Constellation with the false Uruguayan markings CX-BGP, was used to drop several incendiary bombs in the

One of four 749As acquired by Transocean Airlines from BOAC; N9830F was later sold to Korean National Airlines as HL-102

Western Airlines merged with Pacific Northern Airlines in 1967 and took over its 749As; N86525, seen here at Anchorage, Alaska, had been bought from Delta

courtyard of the presidential palace. The Constellation was fired on with automatic weapons but flew out to sea, and the bombs were presumably just thrown or pushed out of the passenger entrance door without the benefit of a bomb-sight. A stray bomb set fire to a hut near Port-au-Prince Cathedral, about half a mile from the palace, and one person was killed and another injured in the fire, but the bombs that landed in the palace courtyard did no damage.

A day after this raid, the same Constellation landed out of fuel at Gold Rock Creek Airport, on the island of Grand Bahama, with the leader of this latest invasion attempt against Haiti, Colonel René Juares Leon, on board with another of his countrymen, seven Americans and a Canadian. The pilot asked to be refuelled but was refused, whereupon all ten men took a taxi into Freeport at the end of the island, leaving their aircraft unguarded (it was later impounded). They were arrested by the police as illegal immigrants, and it is believed that they were either on their way back from the original raid, having made an intermediate landing at some other Caribbean island unannounced, or were returning from an abortive second raid.

The Dominican airline Aerovias Nacionales Quisqueyanas, next door to Haiti, acquired an ex-Eastern Model 649 from the Peruvian operator Copisa (Compania Peruana Internacional de Aviacion SA) to operate passenger services to San Juan from Santo Domingo and charter flights; Copisa had itself acquired this aircraft from Admiral Airways and the Dominican airline also had a Model 049 leased and a 749. Copisa had acquired its first L-749A, an ex-BOAC aircraft sold to Capitol Airways, from California Airmotive in February 1966. Another came to them from Royal Air Maroc of Casablanca in August 1967 and yet another from Bolivia. With these

Copisa operated a service from Iquitos to Maracaibo (Venezuela) and Miami.

Three more 749s were purchased by Trans-Peruana (Cia de Aviacion Trans-Peruana SA) and two other Peruvian operators acquired ex-Eastern Connies. RIPSA (Rutas Internacionales Peruanas SA), which ran cargo flights to Panama and Miami, obtained one from Paramount in September 1966, while LANSA (Lineas Aereas Nacionales SA) took delivery of the first of six 649s and 749s at the end of December 1963, a seventh being bought later for spares and cannibalised. These began operating a domestic network the following month linking Lima with seven other cities, and were later joined by an ex-Qantas L-1049E Super Constellation on lease. Late in 1965 Eastern took a 33·3 per cent holding in LANSA in return for a technical and managerial assistance contract. In May 1966, following the loss of a 649 in an accident in which all on board were killed, operations were suspended until September while LANSA was reorganised as a completely Peruvian company with the Eastern holding bought out. The domestic routes were then resumed and, on the introduction of four Japanese NAMC YS-11A turboprops in April 1967, the Connies were gradually phased out.

Aeronaves de Mexico operated three ex-Air-India 749s during 1958–60 pending delivery of its Britannia 302s and two of these were later leased by International Aircraft Services to Miami Airlines, another 'non-sked', which also had a third 749A on loan from Transocean Airlines which, in turn, was leased by Loftleidir of Iceland during July-August 1960. Transocean had been one of the largest US non-scheduled or supplemental carriers during the 1950s and had operated DC-4s, a DC-6A, 749As, L-1049H Super Constellations and finally Stratocruisers before it went out of business in 1960. It acquired the first of four 749As and

749s from BOAC late in 1957, but these were put up for sale at Oakland in 1959. One of these, N9830F, was sold on 31 July 1959, as HL-102, to Korean National Airlines, a private enterprise operator that was succeeded three years later by the wholly Government-owned Korean Airlines. HL-102 took over the Seoul–Hong Kong route from Korean's DC-4s but this route was discontinued in 1963 (to be reopened four years later with a Super Constellation) and HL-102 was sold as OE-IFE to the Austrian charter operator, Aero Transport Flugbetriebsgesellschaft, which also had an ex-TWA 049 and later bought a 749A from Skyways.

Aero Transport ceased operations in the summer of 1964 after one of its Connies had been impounded for debt at Vienna's Schwechat Airport, the company having previously been involved, late in 1963 and quite legally, in flying arms cargoes to the Yemeni royalists fighting the Egyptians. Another concern which had a somewhat chequered career was the US 'non-sked' World Wide Airlines mentioned earlier, which at various times had four ex-TWA 049s, an ex-TWA L-1049A and two former BOAC 749As on lease. One of the latter had served Capitol Airways, which had three other 749As, having purchased the first from Avianca in 1957; Capitol later built up a fleet of a dozen Super Constellations and went on to operate DC-8 jets. The last US charter operator to acquire a used Constellation was Central American Airways

Flying Service of Louisville, Kentucky, to whom TWA disposed of a 749A in October 1967.

By the 1960s used Connies were being acquired mainly for charter work, but their earlier purchasers in the 1950s had found them every bit as valuable for scheduled services, especially as they were often an operator's first pressurised type. Pacific Northern Airlines acquired three ex-Chicago & Southern 749As from Delta in 1955 after the latter's merger with C & S. These were followed by three more from BOAC and two from TWA, and all were used on PNA's routes from Portland and Seattle to Anchorage and other points in Alaska. Two more ex-KLM 749As were acquired on lease from Aviation Financial Services at the beginning of 1957 but were later returned to KLM as the Constellation fleet built up, and an ex-Eastern 649 was leased from California Airmotive for a year from 8 May 1961. Pacific Northern merged with Western Air Lines on 1 July 1967, the latter operating an extensive network in the western half of the States from Los Angeles. Western then took over PNA's remaining six Constellations but disposed of them all by the end of 1968 when its Boeing 737s were delivered. Two, N86524 and N86525, later found their way to Africa for the Biafra airlift a few months

Used aircraft dealer, International Aircraft Services, owned this 749A N5596A when it was fitted with the rear fuselage section and freight doors of R7V-2 131630 by Lockheed Aircraft Service International

before the Nigerian victory, the former acquiring the bogus Nigerian registration 5N-86H. And, as mentioned earlier, another was used to bomb Port-au-Prince. Wien Alaska Airlines also acquired an ex-KLM 749A in May 1964 for its Fairbanks-based routes; the airline was later known as Wien Air Alaska and became Wien Consolidated Airlines in April 1968 after its merger with Northern Consolidated Airlines.

Air France disposed of some of its surplus Constellations to its associate airlines in Africa. Air Algérie acquired the first of four such 749As late in 1955 (another was also leased) and began services with them early in 1956 linking the major Algerian centres of population to Paris, Marseilles, Toulouse and other French cities. One of these 749As, F-BAZE, was blown up by the OAS on 26 April 1962 as it stood outside a hangar at Algiers' Maison Blanche airport, but there were no casualties. Air Algérie withdrew its last Constellation from service in 1963.

Five more ex-Air France 749As went to Royal Air Maroc, the first in 1957, and with these the airline inaugurated, on 2 July 1958, services linking Casablanca and other places in Morocco to Paris and other cities in France and neighbouring European countries. Two of the 749As were fitted with forward freight doors and these operated an all-freight service from Casablanca to Paris non-stop, while another of the airline's activities was the annual transport of pilgrims to the holy city of Mecca in Saudi Arabia. Two of the 749As were later used for ground training, and

the last was sold to Peru in 1967; another had been leased during 1962–64 to the multi-national airline, Air Afrique, which Air France and the French independent UTA had done so much to set up. And in 1966 Air France 749A F-BAZL was sold to the Senegal Government as 6V-AAR.

In South America, Constellations took over an old-established flying-boat operation when CAUSA—(Compania Aeronautica Uruguaya SA), which had operated Short Sandringhams across the River Plate from Montevideo and Colonia to Buenos Aires since the end of the war, acquired the first of three ex-KLM 749As in February 1963 to replace the Sandringhams, which had become too expensive to operate and maintain, even though they offered a quicker service than landplanes between the city centres.

Other South American acquisitions included a 749A freighter, registered CX-BHC, by a charter operator, Aerolineas Uruguayas SA, and, in March 1964, an ex-KLM 749A by an Argentine company, Aero Transportes Entre Rios SRL, for use on domestic and international freight charters from Buenos Aires. In January 1968, the Bolivian charter operator, Transportes Aereos Benianos SA of La Paz, acquired an ex-Skyways 749A freighter for its cargo flights, but sold it later the same year to Copisa. Finally, an ex-TWA 749A was purchased late in 1968 from Aero Tech Inc by the 'Discover America' travel club, one of the many such clubs formed to get the benefit of cheap air travel by operating their own aircraft.

5: The Super Constellation

By the end of 1949, after four years of post-war operations, air transport had been transformed by the rapid growth of international air routes and widespread public acceptance of the new means of travel. Flying was no longer a luxury for the wealthy few, as it had been a decade previously, and no longer was international air transport the preserve of a small handful of operators like Pan American and Imperial Airways. Already US domestic operators like Capital Airlines had introduced the first coach-class services at cheaper fares, and to the general public, at least, the prospect of mass air travel beckoned invitingly. For manufacturers like Lockheed and Douglas, however, the outlook was far from clear. Both were well aware that stretched versions of their basic Constellation and DC-6 designs would make for reduced costs per seat-mile and so allow of lower fare levels, and clearly there would be a worthwhile market for such stretched versions. But the question facing both as the new decade dawned was how far into the 1950s would it be before jet airliners like the de Havilland Comet made such stretched versions uncompetitive? The Comet had made its first flight on 27 July 1949 and the four-jet Avro Canada C.102 Jetliner a fortnight later, but the jet's operating costs were still rather an unknown quantity, and while their higher speed and cruising altitudes would have obvious passenger appeal, it seemed unlikely that any of the first generation jets would be able to match the low seat-mile costs of piston-engined airliners, especially in the stretched versions. All things considered, it seemed that there was still time for one more round of re-equipment by the airlines with stretched versions of existing types of aircraft before the jets and turboprops took over.

The Constellation had ample reserves of power and this had made possible a series of weight and payload increases from the Model 049 to the 749A but, as the projected Models 749B and 849 had demonstrated, more powerful engines by themselves would result in only marginal improvements as the basic airframe was by now volume limited. What was needed was some fuselage stretch to use the extra power promised by the Turbo-Compound to the best advantage, as well as to achieve higher performance for first-class flights and extra cabin length for the high-density coach-class interiors that were going to be increasingly needed. Flight tests of a Model L-749 at an all-up weight of 137,000lb had indicated the practicability of a 50,000lb payload version of the Constellation, and design studies of just such a version, designated Model L-949, went ahead during 1949. This was intended as a heavy military or civil transport version of the 749 with the fuselage lengthened by 12ft but otherwise similar to the earlier model. It was to be capable of seating up to 100 passengers in an air-coach layout or being used solely as a freight carrier, especially in a military role; maximum gross weight was to be 123,000lb and the designated powerplants were four 2,250bhp (maximum take-off) R-3350 Turbo-Compounds. The Berlin air-lift and the imminence of the Korean war were to stimulate interest in the type's freight-carrying possibilities and one such all-cargo version of the basic 749, known as the Air Freighter, was proposed at about the same time as the Model 949. It was to be fitted with four 2,400bhp (maximum take-off) Pratt & Whitney R-2800 Double Wasps and have a total freight hold volume of 3,750cu ft. US Navy interest in a freighter subsequently resulted in an order for the R7V-1 Super Constellation with freight doors fore and aft, but it was to be several years later before a civil development for freighting was ordered by Seaboard & Western Airlines.

The Model L-1049A Super Constellation

That a short fuselage Constellation could be successfully test flown at an all-up weight no less than 30,000lb greater than that of the Model L-749A demonstrated the degree of stretch there was in the basic design, and the Model 949 was soon superseded by the Model L-1049A Super Constellation with a fuselage lengthened by 18ft $4\frac{3}{4}$in. This increased length was made up of two constant-diameter sections added fore and aft of the spars, the forward section

Eastern Air Lines Model 1049As on the ramp at Burbank prior to delivery

being 128·8in long × 139·3in diameter immediately forward of the front spar, and the rear section, 92in long × 136·6in diameter, added about 55in aft of the rear spar. This extra fuselage length resulted in a cabin 56ft long, 40ft of which had an inside diameter of more than 127in; total length was now 113ft 4in. The circular cabin windows of the short fuselage models were replaced by rectangular windows measuring 16in × 18 in, and a new windscreen, made up of seven flat panels 3½in higher than before, was fitted. To cater for the extra fuselage length and increased cruising speed the structure was strengthened at the cost of very little increase in weight thanks to Lockheed's newly-developed integrally-stiffened skin panel manufacturing techniques. Provision was also made for the installation of centre-section fuel tanks of 730 gal capacity. Of the twenty-four Model L-1049As built, fourteen were Model 1049A-53-67s for Eastern Air

Lines and ten were Model 1049A-54-80s for TWA. The TWA aircraft incorporated the centre-section tanks, whereas those of Eastern only had structural provision for them, and an 88-passenger interior compared with the 75-passenger cabin layout of TWA's aircraft.

The Model 1049A could really be regarded as an interim version incorporating the fuselage stretch and more powerful 'conventional' engines pending the availability of Turbo-Compounds and—later on—the hoped-for installation of turboprops when these became available for commercial use. It was powered by four 2,700bhp (maximum take-off) Wright R-3350-956C18CA-1 powerplants, later redesignated R-3350-956C18CB-1; an alternative version of this engine which could be fitted was the 2,800bhp (maximum take-off) R-3350-975C18BA-1. But the Model 1049A was stressed for the future installation of turboprops of up to 3,500hp such as the Allison T38, which had been used to re-engine the prototype Convair 240 which first flew with these powerplants on 29 December 1950. At this stage Eastern Air Lines was keen to re-engine not only its fourteen Model L-1049A and sixteen Model L-1049C Super Constellations with suitable turboprops when these became available, but also the sixty twin-engined Martin 4-0-4s it then had on order. As an Eastern press release of 17 July 1951 stated:

> When the 3250 horsepower combination reciprocating-turbine 'compound' engines are installed, the Super Constellation's cruising speed will step up to 350 miles an hour and the final conversion to jet power to drive the propellers will advance it well over the 400 mile per hour rating. . . . Installation of the jet power plants driving propellers will raise the speed of these airliners (Martin 4-0-4s) also into the 400 miles-an-hour class of the Super Constellations.

Yet for various reasons, and in spite of the much larger military backing accorded to this form of powerplant in the USA than in Britain during the 1950s, a US turboprop for re-engining the Super Constellation was not to materialise in time, and it was left to Napier to set the pace in this field with the Eland. The 'CB-1 engines of TWA's L-1049As were modified slightly from the normal design to simplify conversion to compound motors if desired by adding an auxiliary unit containing the exhaust-driven turbine to the rear of the engine. And in 1954 TWA requested a number of modifications to their Model 1049As to give a speed increase of approximately 12mph at 20,000ft under long-range cruising conditions. These included extension of the engine nacelles, elongation of the wing/fuselage fillets, rearward extension of the spinners and improvements to the shape of the cowling, closing of one of the three wing intakes for cabin cooling air and reducing a second intake in size, and removing the wing walkway paint.

The 1049A's fuel capacity was increased to 6,550 US gal and its maximum gross weight had gone up to 120,000lb, which was still some way from the full weight limits of the stretched fuselage. Fin area had been increased slightly to counteract the extra length, and drag reduced by removing a number of external excrescences such as the dorsal astrodome that had featured on earlier models; ailerons were now metal-covered. Cabin pressurisation was improved to maintain a cabin altitude of 5,000ft at 20,000ft, and both cabin heating and cooling capacity were substantially increased. An entirely new electrical system was introduced, as well as a new combinaiton electrical-pneumatic de-icer system featuring an electrically-heated strip located along the stagnation line of the leading edges and small high-pressure pneumatic tubes extending aft to the 10 per cent chord line of the wing. More baggage loading doors were also provided, and a fourth optional cargo door could be fitted aft on the Super Constellation, which now had 728 cu ft of underfloor freight space. Altogether, some 550 design improvements went into the first long-fuselage version.

The Re-Birth of 'Old 1961'

'Old 1961', the prototype Constellation, had been bought back by Lockheed from Howard Hughes early in 1950 for conversion into the Super Constellation prototype, and this was done by cutting up the existing fuselage to insert the sections of extra length fore and aft of the wing spars, the circular windows of its original form being retained. Re-registered N67900, 'Old 1961' made its first flight as a Super Constellation at the Lockheed Air Terminal at Burbank on 13 October 1950 and for over a year was engaged in a test programme involving aerodynamic evaluation and development of the control system, powerplant and supercharger development and radio trials. CAA certification trials were completed in only ten weeks, largely with the first two production aircraft for Eastern, N6201C and N6202C. The former had been fitted with six pairs of water-ballast tanks in the cabin for varying the load and c.g. position, and the airscrew blades were strain-gauged to measure vibration. The other production aircraft, N6202C, was fully furnished with eighty-eight passenger seats and was used for testing systems such as hydraulics, electrics and air conditioning. The Super Constellation was certificated on 29 November 1951 at a maximum gross weight of 120,000lb, or 4,000lb more than guaranteed, and met or exceeded all its performance guarantees. Before the prototype flew, sixty-two Model 1049s, valued at $96,041,000, had been ordered by five airlines, and over a hundred by the time the first production aircraft flew, giving Lockheed the largest backlog of orders in its history.

With certification trials out of the way, 'Old 1961' was used to test a number of new features and powerplants intended for future Constellation developments. Early in 1952 it was fitted with two 600 US gal wing-tip tanks, each with a horizontal stabilizing fin at the rear, of the type later to be fitted to the Model L-1049G and

The Super Constellation prototype, 'Old 1961',
with two 600 US gal wing-tip tanks

Model L-1049Es converted to Super G standard,
although for these models and military versions the
horizontal fins were deleted. Originally intended to
cater for the anticipated higher fuel consumption of
turboprop engines (for such versions of the Super
Constellation Lockheed at this stage envisaged not only
tip tanks but two 500 US gal under-wing tanks), the
tip tanks instead became a means of extending range
and their endplate effect was aerodynamically beneficial. Later in 1952 'Old 1961' was fitted with the large
dorsal and ventral radomes of the US Navy's WV-2

'Old 1961' was later fitted with the dorsal and
ventral radomes of the WV-2

early warning version of the Model 1049, the ventral
radome being of greater diameter (about 19ft) than
that of the earlier PO-1W, as well as deeper. In this
configuration it was used for aerodynamic tests of the
radome shape and the interior was not fitted out like
that of production WV-2s.

Shortly before the radomes were fitted a 3,250bhp
(maximum take-off) Wright R-3350-972TC18DA-1
Turbo-Compound was test run in the port outer
nacelle, and a second engine of this type was later
fitted in the starboard outer position; these being the
powerplants intended for the Model L-1049C. After
a time the dorsal and ventral radomes and tip tanks were
removed and, early in 1954, the 'DA-1 Turbo-
Compound in No 4 position was replaced by one
3,750ehp (maximum take-off) Allison YT-56 turbo-

prop which, in its production form, was to power the Lockheed C-130 Hercules military transport. 'Old 1961' made its first flight with the YT-56 on 29 April 1954 and at this stage was flying with a 'DA-1 Turbo-Compound in No 1 position and two ordinary R-3350s inboard. With the Wright engines two types of Curtiss Electric and three models of Hamilton Standard airscrew were tested.

The YT-56 drove a three-blade Curtiss turbo-electric airscrew with broad-chord blades, and the engine was later modified to resemble the civil Allison 501D-13 turboprop which powered the Lockheed Electra. In this form it completed 207 hours flying time, and when the test programme was completed at the end of 1956, it was replaced by a genuine Allison 501D-13 which first flew in 'Old 1961' in March 1957, with an Aeroproducts 606 four-blade airscrew. Four of these powerplants were later fitted in place of the Pratt & Whitney T-34s in an R7V-2 Super Constellation, which became known as 'Elation' in its new role as a flying testbed for Electra engines and systems. Incidentally, it is interesting to recall that in 1955–56 Lockheed were considering the Rolls-Royce RB.109 Tyne and Napier Eland turboprops as possible future engines for the Super Constellation despite the massive test and production programme then being planned for the Allison 501.

After completing Allison 501 testing for the Electra, 'Old 1961' was put into storage and later bought by California Airmotive and eventually broken up. The nose up to the leading edge of the wing was used to repair Air France Model 749A-79-46 F-BAZI which had crashed at Gander, Newfoundland, on 25 August 1954. Its remains were bought by T.O. Associates, who acquired 'Old 1961's' nose for building on to it, but repairs were never completed although the registration N2717A was allotted to the rebuilt aircraft. Thus ended a remarkably interesting career, for 'Old 1961' was certainly unique in being powered at one and the same time by piston engines, a Turbo-Compound and a turboprop.

First Turbo-Compound Version

The outbreak of the Korean war in June 1950 and the USSR's possession of nuclear weapons stimulated two new lines of Super Constellation development; one a long-haul cargo and troop transport for the US Navy, designated R7V-1 (or Model L-1049B), that could, if necessary, mount an airlift across the Pacific, and the other the WV-2 and RC-121 airborne early warning variants. For the former requirement the existing maximum gross, landing and zero fuel weights of the Model 1049A were not adequate and the structural design of the latter's wing had been stretched as far as practical; further increases in gross weight meant

'Old 1961' was fitted in 1954 with a 3,750 eshp Allison YT-56 turboprop in No. 4 position

major structural changes in the wing as well as the extra power of Turbo-Compounds. The wing structure was redesigned so that skin panels and their rib supports could be integrally machined from a slab of 75ST aluminium alloy, thus making it possible to increase the maximum gross weight to 130,000lb, or 10,000lb more than the 1049A's, while keeping the landing weight to 110,000lb, or 7,000lb more than the earlier model's.

The fuselage structure was also redesigned to take large cargo doors fore and aft and a heavy freight floor made up of extruded magnesium planks incorporating cargo tie-down rings, seat attachments and stretcher fittings for casualty evacuation. This floor could take a

The YT-56 was replaced three years later by an Allison 501D-13 turboprop driving an Aeroproducts 606 airscrew; the reduction gear is now below the power section

unit loading of 300lb per sq ft, a value on a par with contemporary warehouse flooring practice and much higher than that of most other freighter aircraft. The floor assembly was sealed to make it possible to hose down the aircraft's interior—which would have been a useful asset in a Berlin airlift type of operation involving the flying of cargoes such as coal or flour—and the cabin walls were lined with fibreglass and had rings for attaching cargo nets. There were two upward-opening freight doors, the forward one measuring 5ft 1½in wide × 6ft 4¾in high and the rear one 9ft 4½in wide × 6ft 2in high. The interior could be fitted out to seat up to 106 passengers in rear-facing 20G removable seats or seventy-three stretcher cases, plus four medical attendants. Alternatively, 38,000lb of freight could be carried in the all-cargo role, quick convertibility from one role to another being a feature of the interior design.

The prototype R7V-1, BuAer 128434, made its first flight on 12 November 1952 with a flight test crew of nine on board and the following March successfully flew at a maximum weight of 145,000lb as part of a test programme for the Hamilton Standard airscrews. An initial order for eleven R7V-1s was placed and the first deliveries were made that same month to the Navy's Fleet Logistics Air Wing for use across the Atlantic and for trans-Pacific operations with the Military Air Transport Service. Altogether, fifty R7V-1s were ordered, but thirty-three of these were transferred to the US Air Force in June 1958 as C-121Gs, those remaining with the Navy being redesignated C-121Js. Late production R7V-1s were delivered with a take-off weight increased to 133,000lb. Powerplants were four

3,250bhp (maximum take-off) Wright R-3350-34W Turbo-Compounds which gave a cruising speed of up to 335mph.

R7V-1 BuAer 131624, named *Phoenix 6*, was specially modified as part of an international research programme into the ecology of Antarctica to catch insects in flight between New Zealand and that continent, being fitted with a special trap to catch the insects without killing them. Two R7V-1s, BuAer 131642 and 131658, which had become C-121Gs with the respective serial numbers 54-4065 and 54-4076, were acquired as transports by NASA for use by the Goddard Space Flight Centre at Greenbelt, Maryland, which operated them with the respective serials NASA 20 and NASA 21, later NASA 420 and NASA 421; they were later registered (respectively) N420NA and N421NA. Together with two EC-121K Super Constellations and a C-121A, they are used by NASA for satellite ground station calibration and downrange instrument checking, an unspectacular but necessary part of the vast US space programme. And since 1966 several C-121Js have been specially converted for TV telecasting duties in Vietnam.

The success of the Navy's R7V-1s stimulated US Air Force interest in a very similar version of the Super Constellation with the same passenger capacity and convertibility to freighting or casualty evacuation. This was the Model L-1049F or C-121C, the new model suffix letter denoting structural reinforcement for a slightly higher maximum gross weight of 137,500lb. Up to 106 passengers in forward-facing or rear-facing seats or seventy-three stretcher cases, plus four medical attendants, or 40,000lb of freight could be

First Turbo-Compound version of the Super Connie was the R7V-1, the prototype of which, BuAer 128434, is seen here

carried, though more typical loads were seventy-five passengers or forty-seven stretcher cases. The folding seats can be stowed in the under-floor freight holds when cargo alone is carried. Four 3,250bhp (maximum take-off) R-3350-91 Turbo-Compounds were fitted and, unlike the R7V-1, the C-121C has a 50hp Solar Mars gas turbine as an auxiliary power unit to provide a source of power when on the ground. An initial order for ten C-121Cs was placed in 1951 and twenty-three more were ordered in 1954; but the first C-121C did not make its maiden flight until July 1955, as production priority had been given to R7V-1s and RC-121 early warning versions. Later thirty-three R7V-1s were turned over to the USAF as C-121Gs. By 1965 the C-121C was being used mainly by US Air National

C-121G NASA 420, used by the NASA's Goddard Space Flight Centre

Guard units in the casualty evacuation role, with ANG squadrons operating a total of fifty-two C-121 Super Connies.

The Model L-1049D Freighter

A commercial freighter based on the R7V-1 would have obvious attractions to those airlines—few as yet—whose volume of freight traffic would justify such an aircraft. The first such version was known as the Model L-1049B and Seaboard & Western Airlines (later to become Seaboard World Airlines) placed an order for four of these at the end of 1951 at a cost of some $10,000,000 including spares. This version had a maximum gross weight of 130,000lb but it was superseded by the Model L-1049D (otherwise identical except for the gross weight being raised to 133,000lb like the late production R7V-1s) and Seaboard & Western switched its order to this variant, which had an airframe stressed for an eventual gross weight of 150,000lb when re-engined with suitable turboprops. The maximum landing weight was now 110,000lb. The 1049D was the world's largest commercial cargo transport when it appeared and it could carry a payload of up to eighteen short tons on the North Atlantic routes, or up to twenty racehorses in individual stalls with their water, hay and feed, although horses if placed too close together are apt to bite each other's

tails through boredom during a long flight, and it would be rare for as many as twenty to be flown at once. The 1049D's maximum payload was 38,570lb and the total cargo hold volume was 5,568cu ft, the main hold being 83ft long. There were fewer cabin windows than on the Model L-1049C.

The same freight doors and heavy-duty magnesium floor as on the R7V-1 were features of the 1049D, which could also incorporate, as an optional 'extra', an electrically-operated mechanical conveyor in the floor to move cargo down the hold. With a maximum full-load speed of 15ft/minute, this conveyor could handle items of freight weighing approximately 12,000lb, or 18,000lb loads at 12ft/minute. The 1049D could also be used as a passenger aircraft, with high-density seating for up to 109 in a coach-class layout, and Seaboard took advantage of this to lease three 1049Ds to BOAC for the New York–Bermuda route during 1955–56. Seaboard had operated the first commercial Atlantic all-cargo flight with a DC-4 on 10 May 1947

and took delivery of its first 1049D N6501C *American Air Trader* on 19 August 1954, three others following in September.

On 19 May 1954 the CAB awarded Seaboard a five-year certificate for a transatlantic route from New York to Germany and Switzerland. The 1049Ds started Atlantic freight charters on 14 September but scheduled services over this route were not inaugurated until 10 April 1956 because of delay in obtaining Presidential approval and traffic rights. DC-4s were used at first but the 1049Ds took over from 1 December, 1956, the US terminals being New York, Philadelphia and Baltimore, with London, Paris, Frankfurt, Hamburg and Zurich the major European terminals. Three 1049Ds were leased to BOAC and flown as 86-passenger aircraft on the New York–Bermuda route from the summer of 1955 to April 1956, after which British West Indian Airways Viscounts took over this route. One 1049D was also leased to Eastern late in 1956 for the New York–Miami holiday traffic, and Seaboard 1049s operated London–New York all-freight services on charter to BOAC from 1958.

One 1049D, N6503C *Paris Air Trader*, was later fitted with wing-tip tanks, and N6501C and N6502C were both modified up to Model L-1049H/03 standard in the summer of 1956 with the higher gross weight of 135,400lb to bring them up to the standard of the five Model L-1049Hs that Seaboard had ordered. This modification programme was undertaken by Lockheed Aircraft Services International and involved the fitting of two 600 US gal tip tanks and four 3,250bhp (maximum take-off) Wright R-3350-972TC18DA-3 Turbo-Compounds in place of the R-3350-972TC18

Seaboard 1049D N6503C was leased to BOAC with two others for the latter's New York–Bermuda route in 1955–56. Note the fewer cabin windows than the 1049C, only eight on the port side

Wartime mockup of rear lounge area for the Constellation with maps and sofa foreshadowing the later Dreyfuss-styled interiors

Lounge area of the Henry Dreyfuss-styled 59-passenger 'Inter-Continental' interior for the 1049C with travel map murals, wood bulkheads and a window-facing 'observation sofa'

DA-1 engines of the 1049D. Subsequently, Seaboard itself increased the gross weight of these 1049Ds to the 137,500lb of the Model L-1049H. In their first full year of operating from 1954, Seaboard's 1049Ds achieved a daily utilisation of 9·9 hours each, and these aircraft also did a good deal of military charter flying.

The First Civil Turbo-Compound
Preceding the 1049D by nearly two years was the first civil Super Constellation with Turbo-Compound engines, the Model L-1049C with four 3,250bhp (maximum take-off) Wright R-3350-972TC18DA-1 radials. These engines could give 3,500bhp for take-off with water-methanol injection, and enabled more load to be carried at higher speeds. The maximum gross weight was 133,000lb, or 13,000lb more than the earlier Model 1049A; the landing weight was 110,000lb and maximum zero fuel weight 103,500lb. The

Model 1049C was offered with a variety of luxury interiors designed by the Henry Dreyfuss organisation to avoid the 'furnished corridor' effect that was becoming increasingly evident in the stretched versions of existing piston-engined airliners. Additional compartmentation was employed to break down this tunnel effect and a new lounge concept was introduced which gave more flexibility in group arrangements for just two people or several. Wood panelling was used extensively, incorporating maps and other travel motifs, and direct diffused lighting with controlled intensity and compartment switching was featured in addition to the usual individually adjustable passenger reading lights. Designed to combine serviceability with an impression of luxury, these interiors were known, respectively, as the 'Inter-Continental', seating 54–60 passengers, the 'Siesta' for 47 passengers in a luxury layout, and the 'Inter-Urban' for 106 people in a high-density coach-class arrangement. A lounge seating up to eight people in high-backed chairs or low-backed two-place sofas facing forward or facing each other could be featured, and this could be curtained off from the rest of the cabin. Other interiors could seat 63, 82, 94 or 97 people and, if desired, freight could be carried in the forward part of the cabin.

Like the 1094D, the Model 1049C was stressed for an eventual gross weight of 150,000lb and its fuel capacity of 6,550 US gal was the same as the 1049A's. The prototype Model L-1049C, PH-TFP *Atoom* (later PH-LKP) for KLM, made its two-hour maiden flight on 17 February 1953. Its cabin was filled with test instrumentation and equipment, and it was flown by Lockheed pilots John Fales and C. P. Nicholson, with P. Jensen and J. Costa as flight engineers. The Dutch airline had ordered nine 1049Cs, but the last four of these were changed to L-1049Es and a tenth was ordered to replace one that crashed at Shannon on 5 September 1954. A repeat order for three more L-1049Es was placed in mid-1952.

KLM's Super Constellations were fitted with Curtiss Electric 858 airscrews with extruded, hollow steel blades which were interchangeable with the Curtiss Electric 830 airscrew blades used on the Model L-749As of KLM and other operators; Hamilton Standard Hydromatic propellers could be fitted as an alternative. In 1955 a modification to its 1049E airscrews was carried out by KLM at its Schiphol workshops to add some 5mph to the speed, as well as improving cooling both in flight and on the ground. This took the form of extending the blade width down to the boss by means of fillets of foam plastic on the blade trailing edge, the blades being subjected to heat, the plastic applied and subsequently hardened in an oven. The process was completed by adding a layer of sheet rubber followed by a coat of paint as a protection against the atmosphere. A special KLM-designed galley was also fitted to its 1049Cs and 1049Es, another refinement being the fitting of loudspeakers instead of headphones for the pilot and navigator. Several interiors were fitted in KLM's 1049Cs and 1049Es, ranging from a 57-passenger layout for the Amsterdam-Johannesburg route, a 52-seat three-class interior (seven de luxe, thirty first-class passengers and fifteen tourists) for the Amsterdam–Sydney route and a high-density 94-passenger 'steerage' interior in four 1049Es for a series of flights carrying immigrants from Amsterdam to Perth, in Western Australia.

The Model L-1049E previously mentioned emphasises that the same process of progressive weight improvements that characterised the Models 649 and 749 was being applied to the Super Constellation, the 1049E being the same as the 1049C with the same maximum take-off weight of 133,000lb. The landing and zero fuel weights were still the same as the 1049C's, but the 1049E incorporated all structural modifications (except to the undercarriage) for an eventual take-off weight of 150,000lb. Some 1049Es were later modified to Model 1049E/01 standard with a maximum take-off weight of 135,400lb or to Model 1049E/02 standard with this same take-off weight and a landing weight increased to 113,000lb. The first production 1049E, YV-C-AMS of Linea Aeropostal Venezolana, made its maiden flight on 6 April 1954 but before the end of that year yet another major variant, the Model L-1049G, or Super G, had been rolled out and it was not long before seven airlines with thirty-eight 1049Es on order had changed over to this later variant. Several other operators had their 1049Es fitted with the 600 US gal tip tanks of the Model L-1049G and modified up to Super G Standard. These included KLM, which had four of its 1049Es so converted from March–June 1956; Iberia of Spain, whose three 1049Es were similarly converted from 1957; Trans-Canada Airlines (now Air Canada) which had two of its 1049E-55s so modified but not fitted with the tip tanks; and Air-India International, which had its three 1049Es thus modified. The two remaining 1049Es of Iberia (a third had been lost in an accident on 6 March 1961) were also converted into freighters in 1963 when they had been finally displaced as firstline equipment by DC-8s. They were also used in the passenger role after this modification on lease to the Spanish independent Aviaco, in particular for holiday charters. A fourth L-1049E was leased by Iberia from KLM from 1 April 1961 to 28 May 1962. Iberia had started Super Constellation services on the Madrid–New York route on 2 September 1954 and later put the type on to its other routes to Latin America and Spanish Africa.

The theme of product improvement started with the short-fuselage Constellations was continued with the 1049 series, particularly through improvements to the production process. From the summer of 1952 the trailing edges of certain wing panels were bonded together with adhesives, thus saving weight, and almost from the start of production 1049s were coming off the production lines at empty weights from 454–942lb less than that specified, the average being 658lb lighter, a bonus that allowed plenty of scope for extra weight in cabin furnishings. A new thermo-plastic interior window frame trimming substance called 'Royalite' was among the first of the minor cabin furnishing and finishing improvements made from time to time.

More evident externally was the installation of cloud- and collision-warning radar from the mid-1950s, both retrospectively and in new aircraft off the production line. Two principal types of radar of this kind were offered for the Super Constellation: the RCA AVQ-10 (5·6cms wavelength) and the Bendix RDR-7 of 3·2cms wavelength, and these could be installed retrospectively by the airline using kits provided by Lockheed. In 1962 Chamberlain Aviation produced two models of its C AIR nose radome for the Constellation, the No 1015 for a 22in fully rotating antenna and No 2015X for an 18in sector scan antenna; both radomes hinged upwards for access to the radar. Weather radar had also been fitted to the C-121A/B Constellations and the two PO-1Ws some time before commercial radars of this kind had been made available. And from 1958, USAF transport aircraft, including C-121s, were fitted with high-intensity collision-warning lights. Following the crash of KLM's 1049E PH-LKY *Triton* at Shannon on 5 September 1954—caused largely by an inadvertent undercarriage re-extension shortly after it had been retracted after take-off, and failure to maintain height with the undercarriage down—it was recommended that the warning lights indicating an unlocked or transient condition of the undercarriage be duplicated, and that self-sufficient emergency lighting for the passenger accommodation be provided.

It was not until fitted with Turbo-Compounds that the Super Constellation began to realise its true potentialities, even though this engine did run into a number of troubles in commercial, and also to some extent, in military service. Of these, the most serious was excessive exhaust flaming and afterburning out of the turbine exhaust hoods of the three 'blown-down' power recovery turbines. Before the engines were modified, the exhaust flames, when the aircraft was climbing, carried right back to the wing trailing edge with adverse effects on structural strength, to say nothing of passenger reaction. Chronic nozzle-box cracking, necessitating many unscheduled removals of turbines and components, together with cooling-cap failures were associated problems that continued even

with the 'DA-3 Turbo-Compounds of the Super G. In 1953 various modifications were put in hand to satisfy the CAA, including the addition of a 2in wide ring of half-inch armour around each turbine, better cooling and detailed changes giving an increased differential between turbine wheel speed (about 19,000rpm) and disc-failure speed. The exhaust flaming problem was not finally beaten until $2,000,000 had been spent on a cure, which took nine months and hundreds of flight tests, while the introduction of new high-temperature materials helped to reduce the unscheduled removal rate resulting from nozzle-box cracking. By 1956 the longest overhaul time on airline Turbo-Compounds was the 1,400 hours achieved by Air France L-1049Cs, whereas two years before the engine was cleared for only 600 hours between overhauls. Oil sedimentation in the clutches was another snag that had to be overcome, but even with the Model L-1049G the engine troubles had not been finally beaten.

The 1049 In Airline Service

But in spite of the headaches it caused the maintenance engineers, the Turbo-Compound in the Super Constellation had the distinction of powering the first non-stop US transcontinental service, the first east-bound non-stop Atlantic flights (with KLM) and the first round-the-world service with Qantas. TWA began Model L-1049A Super Constellation services on 10 September 1952 and inaugurated the first sustained non-stop transcontinental service—named the 'Ambassador'—over the New York–Los Angeles route on 19 October 1953; the westbound flights still stopped at Chicago but eastbound flights made the coast-to-coast journey non-stop in under eight hours. But TWA's competitive edge over American Airlines' DC-6Bs was to be short-lived, for less than six weeks later the latter began Douglas DC-7 services over the same route non-stop in both directions. Eastern Air Lines was the first to inaugurate services with the Super Constellation when it put the 1049A into service on the New York–Miami route on 17 December 1951, and it also ordered sixteen Model L-1049Cs for its major routes, putting these into service two years later. Five of these were converted into freighters by Lockheed Aircraft Services of Ontario, California, during 1959, with big freight doors and heavy-duty floors. The door dimensions were slightly different from those of the Model 1049D and R7V-1, the forward

door being 6ft $0\frac{1}{2}$in high $\times$ 4ft $8\frac{1}{2}$in wide and the rear one 8ft $10\frac{1}{2}$in wide $\times$ 6ft 2in high. A sixth Eastern 1049C was converted into a freighter in 1963.

But it was not as freighters that Eastern's by now nearly obsolete 1049s caught the imagination of the air transport industry and air travelling public alike in 1961. Instead, it was their inauguration of the famous 'Air Shuttle' services between Boston, New York and Washington on 30 April of that year. These no-frills 'walk on' services, although not the first of their kind, were the first really large-scale attempt at a shuttle service, which enabled a cheaper fare to be offered because it cost the airline less to process the passenger. For the travelling public, the attraction was the elimination of the need to check in about thirty minutes before departure, and the ability to buy tickets on board or at the airport. On this service, the passenger pulls a boarding pass out of a machine and writes his name and address on it for the load manifest, and when enough passes had been issued for a full load of ninety-five passengers in Eastern's 1049s the flight was closed out, boarded and dispatched. Back-up aircraft were employed for extra sections of the same flight when there were more than ninety-five people wanting to travel, and on several occasions Eastern laid on a Super Connie to fly virtually empty, carrying only the one or two passengers over the full plane load. Even so, Eastern's 'Air Shuttle' prospered over the years, its network was expanded and Electra turboprops and later DC-9 jets replaced the 1049s; its success was due to a new and welcome emphasis in air transport, on convenience rather than speed.

The First L-1049C Transatlantic Services

KLM was the first to introduce the Model L-1049C, inaugurating the first transatlantic Super Constellation service with this variant on 15 August 1953, scheduling the eastbound flights non-stop from New York to Amsterdam, and offering for the first time a non-stop Atlantic crossing, albeit in only one direction. The Dutch airline was followed by Air France, which began L-1049C flights between Paris and New York on 20 November 1953, and by Trans-Canada Airlines (now Air Canada) which inaugurated L-1049C services on 14 May 1954 from Toronto and Montreal to Glasgow, London, Paris and Dusseldorf. TCA's five L-1049C-55s and three L-1049E-55s featured loud-speakers instead of headphones for the pilots and flight engineer among nearly twenty fairly major and a great many minor modifications; weather radar was fitted from 1957 and later one was used to evaluate the Dectra navigational aid. The 1049Cs and two of the three 1049Es were later modified up to L-1049G standard, but were not fitted with tip tanks. Air France took delivery of ten L-1049C-55-81 Super Constellations and for their first Atlantic services—named 'The Golden Parisian'—eight two-berth sleeping compartments were introduced, the bunks being removed during the day and replaced by two seats. Other low-density interiors featured during the 1950s included a 32-passenger first-class layout, one for twenty-four first-class and thirty-four tourist passengers and, for the 'Eastern Epicurean' services to the Far East, a three-class layout with sleeper, first and tourist accommodation. In 1955 all Air France's Super Constellations were fitted with Kleber-Colombes rubber de-icing boots. And from 1961, after they had been displaced as first-line equipment by Boeing 707s, five of the remaining 1049Cs (which by now had been modified up to L-1049E standard) were converted into freighters similar to Eastern's 1049Cs; one of them was leased to Air Cameroun in 1967.

Air-India had already established its name with the Constellation and it ordered two L-1049Cs and three L-1049Es, the first being delivered in January 1954. With these (and five L-1049Gs ordered later) the existing pattern of routes from London through Europe to India was expanded eastwards, to Singapore via Madras, to Bangkok, Hong Kong and Tokyo and—from 5 October 1956—to Singapore, Darwin and Sydney. A weekly Delhi–Taskhent–Moscow service was started on 1 April 1959 with Super Constellations, although 707s later took over from the 1049s which, in 1962, were disposed of to the Indian Air Force (except for one retained for a time for pilgrim flights to Mecca). Weather radar was fitted from 1958 and, like several

Model 1049E YV-C-AMS of Linea Aeropostal Venezolana was the first production aircraft of this variant

other operators, Air-India adopted the KLM-designed galley for its 1049s. In November 1955 the lounge in Air–India's fleet was removed and replaced by fully-reclining 'slumberette'-type seats for nineteen first-class passengers; the interior was now arranged for thirty-one first-class and forty tourist passengers. Air Ceylon's 'Sapphire' service from Colombo to Amsterdam and London was operated by KLM with a Model L-749A which was replaced in November 1958 by L-1049E PH-LKA *Isotoop*, on lease from the Dutch airline for the next two years; it was later given the Sinhalese registration 4R-ACH and named *Soma Devi*, and after returning from Air Ceylon service it went to Iberia on lease as EC-AQL *La Confiada*.

Three L-1049C Super Constellations formed the fleet of a brand new national airline, Pakistan International Airlines, which began operations with them on 7 June 1954 on the 'inter-wing' services between Karachi and Dacca, the capitals of West and East Pakistan. On 1 February 1955, PIA's 1049Cs began international operations between Karachi and London via Cairo, with what was then the fastest schedule over the route, and after they were displaced as first-line equipment by Boeing 720Bs from 1962 they were put on to the major domestic routes, and in 1966 began operating night air coach services domestically. They were also fitted with weather radar.

Close-up of Turbo-Compounds on an Eastern 1049C

Another major Commonwealth operator of Super Constellations was Qantas, which ordered four L-1049Cs initially in 1951 and six more in April 1953; in 1958 all ten were modified up to L-1049E/01-55 standard, the first one having been delivered on 29 March 1954. They went into service on the trans-Pacific route to San Francisco and Vancouver on 15 May 1954 as well as on the 'Kangaroo' route to London, and on 14 January 1958 Qantas achieved the notable distinction of being the first airline to operate a regular, scheduled service around the world when its Super Constellation service to San Francisco was extended on a twice-weekly basis through New York to London to connect there with the 'Kangaroo' services to Sydney through south-east Asia. Qantas 1049s also took over from 749As the route across the Indian Ocean to Johannesburg on 5 November 1954 and the Sydney–Tokyo route in May 1955. A 1049E was leased to Malayan Airways in 1960 for its Singapore–Hong Kong route.

During 1955 the Qantas aircraft were modified to carry up to 16,000lb of freight and fifty-seven tourist-class passengers with an increased zero fuel weight and some strengthening of the wing root. Other interiors featured were an all first-class layout for thirty-nine passengers and a three-class interior for seven de luxe, twenty first-class and thirty-five tourist passengers; in 1961 Qantas 1049s seated 34–85 passengers. From the start of their life they had been fitted with RAE counting accelerometers and fatigue meters to gather data on gust intensity and fatigue as part of the Australian aviation research programme. And from 1955, following advances in communication techniques, Qantas dispensed with the radio officer as a crew member. Two L-1049E/01-55s were converted into freighters in 1960 by Lockheed Aircraft Services to supplement the two L-1049H freighters already delivered, and with these an all-freight service from Sydney to London was operated. As the Boeing 707s came into service the 1049s were sold off, the last being delivered to a US dealer on 6 May 1963.

In Latin America, two Constellation operators ordered Super Connies: Avianca of Colombia put three L-1049Es into service late in 1954, plus a 1049G two years later; these were put on to the routes from

Bogota to Paris and Frankfurt via Bermuda and Santa Maria in the Azores, and from Bogota to Miami and New York via Kingston or Montego Bay in Jamaica. The accommodation layout was originally for thirty-nine first-class and fifteen tourist passengers but this later gave way to a 64-passenger layout. One 1049E was later converted into a freighter, and like the other remaining (the third had been lost in an accident on 1 January 1960) was modified up to Super G standard. Linea Aeropostal Venezolana put two L-1049Es into service in 1954 on its central Atlantic route from Caracas through Bermuda and Santa Maria in the Azores to Lisbon, Madrid and Rome, and also on the routes to Lima (Peru) from Caracas, to Miami via Havana and to New York non-stop.

One of the first operators to order Super Connies, Braathens South American & Far East Airtransport A/S (SAFE) was prevented from taking delivery by government action, and had to cancel its order. Formed by the airminded Norwegian shipowner Ludvig G. Braathen, who in 1937 had applied to operate an Oslo–London air service and the following year planned a transatlantic service with Boeing 314 flying-boats, Braathens began operating DC-4s after the war to Hong Kong and South America on a non-scheduled basis. Early in 1949 the Oslo–Hong Kong route was put on a regular basis when the Norwegian government authorised Braathens to operate over it for a period of five years, and a weekly DC-4 service began in August 1949, two months before SAS started services to Bangkok, and continued until April 1954. Two L-1049Es were ordered in anticipation of Braathens' operating authority to the Far East being renewed, but in mid-1954 SAS had extended its Bangkok route to Hong Kong and Tokyo and the Norwegian government, as a partner in Scandinavian Airlines System, could not license an independent airline in competition with SAS on an international route. So Braathens' operating authority was not renewed, its Hong Kong route was suspended and the 1049E order was cancelled, the airline thereafter concentrating on Norwegian domestic services and on charters. Altogether, twenty-four Model L-1049As and seventy-four Model L-1049Cs and Model L-1049Es were built.

6: New 1049 Versions and Operators

With the Super Constellation stressed for the future installation of suitable turboprops and with the commercial Turbo-Compound engined versions now capable of an eventual take-off weight of 150,000lb it was natural that a turboprop flight test programme should be initiated as soon as possible. Already airline interest in the new powerplant was evident and Capt Eddie Rickenbacker of Eastern had visited the UK in 1952 to see Comet jet and Viscount turboprop production and development for himself.

In November 1951 the designation Model 1149 had been given to a proposed turboprop conversion of the Model 1049 and the following year design work began on the first all-turboprop Super Constellation to flight-test the Pratt & Whitney T–34 turboprop for the US Navy. Two aircraft on the R7V-1 production line, BuAer 131630 and 131631, were fitted with four 5,500ehp (maximum take-off) Pratt & Whitney YT-34-P-12 turboprops driving three-blade, broad chord, square-tipped Hamilton Standard Turbo-Hydromatic airscrews of 15ft diameter and 2ft chord; designated R7V-2, this new variant made its first flight on 1 September 1954. Two more R7V-2s intended for the Navy, BuAer 131660 and 131661, were later transferred to the US Air Force as (respectively) 53-8157 and 53-8158, being redesignated YC-121F after originally being known as the C-134-LO. The first of these made its maiden flight on 5 April 1955 and for a time flew with its Navy serial but with USAF lettering on the nose.

The YC-121Fs had T-34-P-6 turboprops of 5,700eshp and two 600 US gal wing-tip tanks to give a total fuel capacity of 8,750 US gal; there was also provision (as in the R7V-2) for two 500 US gal underwing tanks, although these were not in fact fitted. Both the R7V-2 and YC-121F had a maximum take-off weight of 150,000lb, a payload of up to 36,000lb, and could cruise at no less than 440mph, making them the world's fastest propeller-driven transports. At the beginning of 1956 an R7V-2 piloted by R. E. Wimmer and J. F. Ware reached a speed of 479mph in a dive, equivalent to the maximum diving speed of the wartime P-38 Lightning fighter; this speed was achieved in the R7V-2 flying from 25,000ft to 8,000ft at an angle of approximately twenty degrees at a low power setting as part of a rapid descent test. At about the same time an R7V-2 took off at a record gross overload weight of 166,400lb—nearly twice the gross weight of the Constellation prototype thirteen years earlier—as part of a programme, like the diving test, to meet the US Navy's 'extreme emergency' specifications, particularly as regards structural strength. For this overload test the R7V-2 carried a full fuel load plus 30,000lb of water in special tanks inside the cabin, lead ballast totalling 7,800lb and 8,214lb of test equipment, a disposable load adding up to over 46,000lb. In production form the R7V-2 and YC-121F would have had the same interiors as the R7V-1 and C-121C, carrying up to 106 passengers overland or 97 over water, or 73 stretcher cases plus four medical attendants, or 36,000lb of freight.

Of the two R7V-2s one was used by Lockheed for performance, stability, control and engine trials and the other for radio, air conditioning, pressurisation, electrical and other systems testing. With the YC-121Fs, they joined four other T-34 test beds, two Boeing YC-97J Stratofreighters and two Douglas YC-124B Globemasters. Yet in spite of this sizeable test fleet further development of the T-34 engine into new versions had ceased by 1954 in favour of later designs and this powerplant was already a decade old. Its development for the US Navy had begun in June 1945 but in the end it only went into production for one aircraft, the Air Force's Douglas C-133 Cargomaster intended to replace the C-124 Globemaster. The T-34 had first flown in the nose of a

Two R7V-2s were used as flying test-beds for the Pratt & Whitney T-34 turboprop, which gave them a cruising speed of 440 mph

B-17 Fortress in August 1950 and by the time it powered the Super Constellation it was no longer representative of the latest design practice. A single-shaft engine with a 13-stage axial-flow compressor and three-stage turbine, it was now up against the new generation of two-shaft engines with separate high- and low-pressure compressors, exemplified by the Rolls-Royce Tyne, with a higher pressure ratio (akin to compression ratio in a piston engine) and hence lower specific fuel consumption.

But in spite of the T-34's age, Lockheed proposed two airline versions powered by this engine, the Model L-1249A freighter based on the Model L-1049D, and the Model L-1249B passenger aircraft similar to the Model L-1049E. These were to be much the same as the civil Super Constellation except for the power-plants, which were Pratt & Whitney PT2F-1s, a civil version of the T-34 also sometimes known as the Turbo-Wasp and giving 5,500ehp for maximum take-off. The engine nacelle attachment points were to be modified for the new engines, and the undercarriage strengthened for a maximum take-off weight of 150,000lb. A maximum speed of 449mph was forecast

for the 1249B, with a cruising speed of 368mph at 25,000ft, and the maximum payload was to be 40,918lb. Two 600 US gal wing-tip tanks would normally have been fitted, with provision for two 500 US gal under-wing tanks, the wing span being reduced to 117ft before the tip tanks were fitted, and increased to 126ft with the tanks in place. The absolute range with all four external tanks would have been 4,150 miles. The Model 1249 could have flown from London to Moscow and back in seven hours, or to Cairo in six hours with a load of 32,000lb, or San Francisco or Los Angeles to Honolulu in under six hours, or New York to London in $8\frac{3}{4}$ hours with a stop at Gander. Had airline interest been sufficient, existing Model 1049s could have been re-engined to become 1249s but in the end the latter model was abandoned through lack of firm orders.

Following flight tests of an Allison YT-56 and then a 501D-13 in 'Old 1961', one of the R7V-2s, BuAer 131631, was obtained by Lockheed on bailment from the US Navy after the T-34 test programme was completed and re-engined with four 3,750ehp (maximum take-off) Allison 501D-13s for a 1,000-hour flight test programme to develop the Lockheed Electra engine and systems. Conversion to the Allison turboprops started at the end of 1956 and the R7V-2 became known as the 'Elation' with its new engines, which drove

Aeroproducts 606 four-bladed airscrews. Like the T-34 installation, the 501D-13 jet pipes exhausted over the wing trailing edges but were of a smaller diameter befitting the less powerful engines. The cowling shape was also different, due to the Allison engine's reduction gearing to the airscrew being offset below the power section. With two Convair YC-131Cs of the MATS 1700th Squadron fitted with 3,250hp Allison YT-56s, the 'Elation' took part in an intensive test programme for Allison turboprops and by July 1958, a year after it had first flown with these powerplants, it had completed more than 750 hours of engine development flying, and was averaging a daily eight hours' simulated airline flying. Yet in spite of what was by European standards a pretty massive flight proving programme, the Allison 501D-13 installation in the Lockheed Electra had a chequered career and encountered a considerable amount of engine and structural trouble.

Another Super Constellation test bed took to the air in France on 2 March 1971 at the Istres Flight Test Centre with a civil version of the new SNECMA-Turboméca M49 Larzac turbofan mounted beneath the fuselage. This engine, of from 2,300lb st to 5,400lb st is intended for executive jets such as the Dassault Falcon 10 and jet trainers such as the Dassault-Dornier Alpha Jet. SNECMA and Turboméca were responsible for the Larzac installation.

After their test programmes had been completed and the time came for them to be broken up all four of the turboprop test Super Constellations were partly rebuilt into other Constellations. The rear fuselage (complete with freight doors) of R7V-2 BuAer 131630 had been rebuilt on to the ex-Air–India and Aeronaves de Mexico Model L-749A LV-IIG (ex-LV-PBH) acquired by the Argentine charter operator Aerolineas Carreras TA in July 1964. After TWA's Model L-1049G N7121C *Star of Edinburgh* suffered a fuselage failure during a pressurisation test on 24 June 1959, it was fitted with the forward fuselage (and freight doors) of the other R7V-2, BuAer 131631, becoming a Model L-1049G/H06 in the process and also acquiring the tail unit of the R7V-2. It had been sold to California Airmotive 'as is' after its accident and they had it rebuilt and then leased it to Trans-International Airlines from 23 April 1961 and later to Standard Airways. By 1963 it had been sold to a firm of car dealers called Bill Murphy Buick Inc, who leased it to the Flying Tiger Line from 1 May 1964 to 28 June 1965.

In 1963 Flying Tiger put into service two 'new' Model L-1049H Super Connies, made by mating the fuselages of YC-121Fs 53-8157 and 53-8158 to the wings, powerplants and tail units of two surplus Linea Aeropostal Venezolana L-1049Gs, respectively YV-C-AMI and YV-C-AME, which had been sold to

Two more R7V-2s were transferred to the USAF as YC-121Fs; the one shown here, later to become 53-8157, retains its Navy serial and has tip tanks

R7V-2 BuAer 131631 was re-engined with four Allison 501D-13 turboprops for the Electra test programme, being known as Elation

California Airmotive. The fuselage of 53-8157 was combined with the rest of YV-C-AMI, the resulting aircraft being registered N173W, and that of 53-8158 with YV-C-AME to become N9749Z and later N174W. The real reason for this apparently expensive rebuild was Flying Tiger's desire to avoid paying the full going price for a Model L-1049H freighter—about $500,000 —and having first obtained the two YC-121Fs the airline then acquired the two ex-Venezuelan Super Gs at knockdown prices, the YC-121F fuselages with their freight doors being similar to the L-1049H's. By the time the first of these rebuilt Super Constellations was completed in July 1963 and the second around the end of the year, Flying Tiger had succeeded in producing two serviceable aircraft from four for less than the price of one new L-1049H. The biggest problem in these rebuilds was adaptation of the electrical systems to a uniform Model L-1049H standard from the differing systems of two separate models. N174W was sold to Interior Airways of Fairbanks, which operate scheduled and charter services in Alaska, on 21 January 1966 but leased back to Flying Tiger on 1 July of that year and bought back by them on 1 January 1968. It was sold the following year to Murphree Air International and in August 1969 to the North Slope Supply Co of Anchorage for air transport support work in support of oil-drilling operations in northern Alaska. N173W was likewise sold to Murphree Air International on 19 December 1968 and to the North Slope Supply Co the following year.

'Columbine III'

After General Eisenhower became President of the United States he continued to use a C-121A for a time as his VVIP transport but this was replaced on 31 August 1954 by VC-121E-LO Super Constellation 53-7885 *Columbine III*; this was originally to have been R7V-1 BuAer 131650 but was completed as the VC-121E. Like the C-121C, the VC-121E featured the rectangular windows of the airline Model 1049s instead of the circular windows (fewer in number) of the R7V-1, but the spacing of *Columbine III*'s windows was slightly different to that of production C-121Cs. A special teletype installation for receiving and transmitting 'classified' messages was a feature of the Presidential aircraft, as were a television set and an air-to-ground radio telephone link which connected the speaker to a special operator on the ground, who then put through a trunk call. In command of *Columbine III* was General Eisenhower's personal pilot, Col William G. Draper, whose crew were hand-picked, and took special precautions when flying the President. Pilot and co-pilot ate their meals at a two hours' interval from each other to minimise the risk of both being simultaneously incapacitated by food poisoning, and all luggage, unless carried by hand, was carefully examined before stowage. Maintenance standards were exceptionally high and after every 1,000 hours of flying *Columbine III* was returned to the Lockheed factory and virtually rebuilt. *Columbine III* served as the Presidential aircraft until January 1961 and was transferred to the USAF Museum in April 1966.

New Operators

Like the Models 049, 649 and 749, the Super Constellation sold steadily in the second-hand airliner market, although fewer new operators bought used Super Connies than had acquired its predecessor, many preferring the used DC-7s that came on to the market during the 1960s. Most of TWA's ten Model L-1049As were in storage in 1960 and the last five were sold to Florida State Tours on 7 August 1964, while Eastern sold eleven of its Model L-1049As to the Aviation Corp of America in 1968. As before, the various US 'non-skeds' were ready buyers. California Hawaiian Airlines acquired two 1049As from TWA in June and December 1960 (leasing one to Modern Air Transport for a time) but both aircraft were attached in April 1962 because TWA had not received full payment of the purchase price, although a third 1049A was leased from TWA at about this time, and had also been leased to General Airways, another 'non-sked,' in 1960–61. The two attached aircraft were later sold to Florida State Tours. One was subsequently disposed of to an Argentine charter operator, Lineas Aereas Patagonica Argentinas SRL (LAPA), and crashed into the sea on 6 March 1966 south of Lima (Peru) while en route for Asuncion (Paraguay) on what transpired to have been a smuggling flight. LAPA also acquired a Model L-1049D freighter from Seaboard World Airlines for its non-scheduled freight services. Another ex-TWA Model 1049A was leased by Paramount Airlines from California Airmotive for a month in 1961 and then went to Modern Air Transport (together with a second 1049A) and was then leased to Standard Airways, returning to California Airmotive in January 1964. Standard also acquired an ex-Trans-Canada Airlines L-1049C-55 through California Airmotive on

3 August 1962 and an ex-TCA L-1049E-55 in 1961 from the same source; the latter had previously been leased to Capitol and was sold to American Flyers on 8 April 1964.

Undoubtedly the most glamorous setting for a second-hand Super Connie operation was that of South Pacific Air Lines, which started a weekly service from Honolulu to Tahiti on 2 April 1960 with a 1049A, N6903C, leased from TWA two months before and named *Bounty* after Capt Bligh's famous ship. Until 20 September 1960 the final Bora Bora-Papéeté sector of this route in the Society Islands was operated by the local French inter-island airline, Reseau Aérien Interinsulaire, with a Short Sandringham flying-boat, as Bora Bora was then the only airport available and the new international airport at Papéeté did not open until October 1960. A second 1049A was purchased from TWA on 7 June 1962, but South Pacific ceased operations after agreeing to lease its Honolulu-Tahiti route to Pan American in September 1963.

South Pacific's choice of 1049As instead of the 1049Cs or Es normally used for long-haul overwater routes was unusual and second-hand 1049Cs did not lack buyers among the US 'non skeds'. Capitol Airways, for instance, acquired one—an ex-Trans-Canada Airlines L-1049C-55—in November 1963, having previously purchased an L-1049E-55 (that later went to Standard), and four ex-Qantas L-1049E/01-55s. Capitol also leased in May 1962 three ex-Seaboard World Model L-1049Ds, two of which they bought in March 1966. American Flyers also operated, in

Model 749 F-ZVMV with anti-icing spray rig on forward fuselage and vee struts for carrying engine

Formerly XA-GOQ of Aerovias Guest and F-BAZR of Air France, 749 F-ZVMV of the French Air Force is used as a test bed for the Turboméca Bastan VII turboprop of the Nord 262. The icing rig forward sprays water into the intake to check the effect of icing on engine handling, and an observation port just aft of the rig enables the intake to be monitored in flight

addition to two ex-Trans-Canada 1049Es, a pair of ex-Qantas Model L-1049E/01-55s, one of which had previously been leased to Trans-International Airlines and later operated by LANSA of Peru on lease for a time.

A Canadian charter operator, Montreal Air Services, also purchased an ex-Trans-Canada L-1049C-55 in 1964 and an L-1049H the following year. Both were later leased to another Canadian charter carrier, World Wide Airways, but the L-1049C was broken up for spares and the L-1049H returned to Montreal Air Services when World Wide's licence was revoked in August 1965. World Wide had also operated another L-1049 and an ex-Qantas L-1049E/01-55 acquired in 1964. The latter was subsequently acquired by the Argentine charter operator Aero Transportes Entre Rios SRL, for its freight operations in South America and the same company later acquired an ex-Seaboard World Model L-1049D freighter and also two Model L-1049Hs. In 1970 it disposed of its Super Connies but retained its Model L-749A. Other Latin American purchasers of second-hand Super Connies included two Panamanian firms, Interamericana Export-Import SA, which bought from International Aerodyne an ex-Iberia L-1049E which was later used on the Biafra airlift, and Aero Fletes Internacional SA, which acquired an L-1049 for its charter work in 1971.

In Europe, the French charter operator Air Frêt added an ex-Air France Model L-1049C and three L-1049Gs from the same source to its fleet, subsequently selling the L-1049C to another French charter operator, Catair, which already owned four other ex-Air France aircraft of the same type, and later a fifth Super G previously operated by Air Cameroun. Air Frêt replaced all but one of its Super Connies in 1970 with three Douglas DC-7BF freighters and one of its Super Gs later went to Phoenix Air Transport, another charter operator.

While most major 1049 operators had to sell off their fleets over a long period, usually to charter operators who sometimes found difficulty in paying for them, Air-India was luckier in that its Super Constellations—two L-1049Cs, three L-1049Es and four L-1049Gs—were all disposed of in 1962 to the Indian Air Force, except for one kept for a time for pilgrim flights to Mecca. Air-India received about £3 million for the nine aircraft, or over £300,000 each, by no means a bad price when many other Super Connies had to be stored and eventually broken up because they could not find a buyer.

The Indian Air Force initially used one of its 1049s as a long-haul transport, while the rest of the fleet were allotted to search and rescue and maritime reconnaissance roles. For this they were later fitted with avionics and other special equipment and they replaced in No 6 Squadron the venerable Consolidated Liberator G.R. VI bombers which the Indian Air Force had previously employed on these duties.

Formerly VH-EAJ Southern Star *of Qantas, 1049E N9718C was sold through Lockheed to 20th Century Aircraft (20th Century Airlines) which leased it and later sold it to Capitol*

*Indian Air Force 1049G BG579 coded 'D' was
formerly Air-India's VT-DJX* Rani of Sagurai
converted into a freighter

7: The Early Warning Versions

Ten weeks before the USSR exploded its first atomic bomb on 22 September 1949, and so added a new dimension to the threat of global warfare, an aircraft specially developed for the US Navy as a flying radar station had made its first flight. This was the PO-1W (later WV-1) and two of these aircraft quickly demonstrated the soundness of the basic concept of an aerial radar picket able to operate at high altitudes and so overcome the limitations imposed by a curving horizon on the straight line transmission of unbending radar beams. Realisation of the full potential of this concept had, however, to await the arrival of the Super Constellation with its more powerful Turbo-Compound engines, longer fuselage and higher gross weight, and development of an AEW (Airborne Early Warning) version of the Model L-1049 began in 1950. Originally known as the PO-2W, it was redesignated WV-2 early in 1952. Also in 1952 'Old 1961', now the Super Constellation prototype, was fitted with the large dorsal and ventral radomes of the WV-2, in addition to its two 600 US gal wing-tip tanks. In this configuration it was aerodynamically representative of the production WV-2, although it did not feature the latter's special interior, and was used to check the effect of the large radomes on control and handling characteristics, the ventral radome, measuring approximately 19 × 29ft, being larger and deeper than that of the earlier WV-1. In production WV-2s this immense radome contained an APS-20B sea search radar, the 8ft-high dorsal radome housing the APS-45 height-finding radar antenna.

Speaking of the production WV-2 and RC-121C, Clarence L. 'Kelly' Johnson, Lockheed's chief engineer, said in 1954: 'This airplane constitutes a picket line at our defence perimeter. And it is likely to be the first American airplane in action if this country should be attacked. These flying radar stations can provide as much as three to five hours warning of an enemy attack against this country—something we never had before. That's the next best to a telephone warning from the enemy himself'. By flying high to overcome the line-of-sight limitations of radar beams that cannot bend over the horizon, the WV-2 and RC-121C could perform five main tasks:

(i) Detect incoming aircraft from any height from the maximum altitude of jet bombers down to the low over-the-ocean flight of strike aircraft, and fix their course and speed long before they neared their targets;

(ii) Function if desired as a combat intelligence centre during amphibious assault operations or fleet actions;

(iii) Direct fighters in aerial combat as they are called up from aircraft carriers or ground bases to intercept enemy aircraft;

(iv) Detect submarines below the surface or ships and call up other aircraft to attack them;

(v) Act as weather reconnaissance aircraft to locate and track weather disturbances, in particular hurricanes in areas like the Caribbean.

The WV-2 carried some 12,000lb of electronics and associated equipment and its crew, ranging in number from twenty-six to thirty-one, included relief pilots, radar operators, technicians and maintenance specialists. Its 3,250bhp (maximum take-off) R-3350-34 Turbo-Compounds and 600 US gal tip-tanks enabled it to remain in the air for over twenty-four hours if necessary, and there were bunks convertible to couches, a galley with refrigerator, running water and grills for the crew's comfort and sustenance. The cabin was pressurised to maintain an altitude of 10,600ft while flying at 25,000ft, and liberally soundproofed to minimise crew fatigue. Even the seats had been specially designed to reduce fatigue to a minimum on long patrols. A high degree of self-containment was aimed at, each WV-2 carrying its own complete electronics maintenance shop with extra electronic tubes, spare parts, tools and work benches for specialist crewmen to make in-flight adjustments and repairs. Details of the strength, speed and number of any enemy attacking force could be transmitted to defending aircraft or missile sites by UHF (ultra high frequency) radio.

Operational nerve centre of the aircraft is the

Combat Intelligence Centre in the central part of the cabin where radar watchers sit, mostly facing aft, at radar consoles engaged in spotting, plotting and directing duties. To the rear of the Centre are five radar search scopes, each with a seat for a crew member, and at the extreme aft end of the cabin there are bunks for the relief crew. Crew members are designated CICO (Combat Intelligence Chief), ACICO 1, ACO 2, 3, 4 and 5, height finder, radar operator, ECM (electronic counter-measures) operator, poster, talker and plotter. The radar consoles and plotting tables in the Centre permit observation of various presentations or segments of the same basic radar picture and work on a variety of search and interception problems, co-ordinating all search information for onward transmission to shore bases, ships or other aircraft, while the auxiliary radar search scopes provide specialised presentations. Both the ventral and dorsal radars are capable of 'seeing' some 200 miles at an altitude of 25,000ft and the navigational equipment includes APS-42 storm-warning radar in the nose and Loran. The crew works in two shifts and to avoid distraction while concentrating on a radar screen there are only a few circular cabin windows and an interior system of controlled intensity lighting. Maximum gross weight of the WV-2 is 145,000lb and the fuel capacity is 7,750 US gal, the tip-tanks being standard and increasing the wing span to 126ft.

WV-2 deliveries began in 1954 and this version entered squadron service with Airborne Early Warning Squadron One (or VW-1 as it was designated) at Pearl Harbour in April of that year; a peculiarly appropriate location since the success of the Japanese attack of 1941 had largely been due to lack of any adequate early warning system against surprise attack. Altogether, 141 WV-2s and one WV-2E were built and five separate orders were placed for it to extend production into 1958.

Early Warning Flight Operations

From 1 July 1956, WV-2s maintained a continuous radar watch of the North Atlantic approaches—known as the 'Barrier Atlantic'—with the first airborne early warning wing of three squadrons (VW-11, VW-13 and VW-15) rotating between Argentia, Newfoundland and Patuxent River, Maryland. During the first nine months an average of 3·7 missions every twenty-four hours were flown from Argentia in some of the worst flying weather in the world but without a single major accident to man or aircraft. Fog and snow conditions were frequent but gale-force winds were the major problem, take-offs often having to be made in winds of over 58mph. One night departure was made in a wind speed of 106mph, and there was an instance of a WV-2 being landed successfully in a 34mph-crosswind.

The WV-2 had been preceded into first-line service by the US Air Force's version of it, the RC-121C, although US Navy interest in the flying radar picket Constellation had been evident some time before the Air Force's. Ten RC-121Cs which had originally been laid down as C-121C transports entered service with the 552nd Airborne Early Warning and Control Wing in October 1953, and this version was very similar to the WV-2, having a total fuel capacity of 6,550 US gal without the tip-tanks, although these could be fitted.

Deliveries of the WV-2 began in 1954 to Squadron VW-1 at Pearl Harbour, and 141 in all were built

EC-121D 0-50133 is a special electronics version with the dorsal radome removed

Motors were four 3,650hp (maximum take-off) R-3350-93 Turbo-Compounds, slightly more powerful than the R-3350-34s of the WV-2. The weather radar in the nose brought the total length to 116ft 2in, and the overall height was 27ft. Like the WV-2, the RC-121C flying at 10,000ft could cover with its ventral radar a surface area of approximately 45,000 square miles during a patrol, according to Lockheed calculations. When it was finally superseded by later versions, such as the RC-121D and EC-121H, several RC-121Cs were converted to the TC-121C convertible passenger/cargo version with radar and electronics removed.

The next USAF version was the RC-121D; deliveries began in May 1954 and seventy-two were built in all. The first aircraft went to the Wright Air Development Centre at Dayton, Ohio, for testing and others initially went into service with the 4701st Airborne Early Warning and Control Squadron of the Eighth Air Division at Sacramento, California. RC-121Ds equipped two wings, the 551st Airborne Early Warning and Control Wing at Otis Air Force Base near Boston, Massachusetts, whose thirty RC-121Ds went into service in March 1955, and the 552nd Airborne Early Warning and Control Wing based at Sacramento, California for Pacific guard duties. The RC-121D differed from the RC-121C in having the two tip-tanks as standard and a fuselage fuel tank of 1,000 US gal capacity to give a total fuel capacity of 8,750 US gal, sufficient for an endurance of twenty-four hours. The fuselage tank necessitated some rearrangement of the interior and was a departure from the original idea of two 500 US gal underwing tanks envisaged for the commercial turboprop-powered Super Constellations. The RC-121D featured new radar consoles with larger viewing scopes for sighting and plotting targets, and for relaxation between watches there were four lounge-type chairs in a crew rest area forward of the Combat Intelligence Centre amidships. There were also eleven bunks available for the off-duty shift, and a galley located in the rear compartment. A special cooling system was developed for the D-series to relieve the heat generated by some 3,000 vacuum tubes in the aircraft's radar and other electronics; apparently over-heating of these had been something of a problem with previous versions. Late in 1957 Lockheed was awarded

The RC-121D, exemplified by 0-23421 seen here, differed from the RC-121C in having a fuselage fuel tank of 1,000 US gal capacity. This aircraft belongs to the 552nd AEW and Control Wing

a $1,536,253 contract for the manufacture and proto-type installation of electronic equipment kits in an RC-121D.

In May 1958 the US and Canadian air defence systems had been formally merged into the North American Air Defence Command—NORAD—and one of its most important tasks was the defence of Strategic Air Command bases, particularly from any Russian attack that might come from over the Arctic. The WV-2s and RC-121s on patrol in the Atlantic or Pacific were extensions of the shore-based radar defences, in particular the famous DEWline chain of radar outposts stretching from Alaska across northern Canada to Greenland, and following the fringe of the Arctic Circle; the Mid-Canada Line extending across the continent; and the Pine-tree Line, which is more or less on the US-Canadian border. In addition to these shore-based radar chains there are 'Texas Tower' radar outposts built at distances of up to 200 miles from the US coastline, and radar picket ships at sea. Information received from these chains of radar outposts was

The EC-121H carries an extra ton of electronics, including an airborne computer, for integration with the SAGE system, and is identified by the smaller dorsal radome ahead of the main one. EC-121H 55-5267 seen here, was formerly WV-2 141318

fed into an electronic weapons control system known as SAGE—Semi-Automatic Ground Environment—which automatically directs fighter squadrons or surface-to-air missiles to ensure that no target is over-looked and no interception duplicated.

The RC-121Ds of the 551st Airborne Early Warning and Control Wing were converted to EC-121H standard during 1963–64, this version carrying an extra ton of electronics, including an airborne computer, to transmit information automatically to SAGE installations on the ground. This version is identifiable externally by a smaller dorsal radome on the forward

The WV-2E (later EC-121L) featured APS-70 radar in a 40ft dish radome which contained the slowly rotating scanner. Only one WV-2E, BuAer 126512, was built

An aerial view of Navy EC-121Ks at the Military Aircraft Storage and Disposition Centre (MASDC) at Davis-Monthan Air Force Base, Arizona, awaiting scrapping or modification

fuselage ahead of the main one, and the maximum weight went up from the 143,600lb of the RC-121D to about 146,000lb. The RC-121s of the 552nd Wing operating over the Pacific were not modified to transmit to the SAGE system. The prefix 'E' in the designation EC-121H denoted 'Special Electronic Installation,' and under the new uniform system of US military aircraft designations established by Department of Defence Directive No 4505.6 dated 6 July 1962, the WV-2 became the EC-121K, as the remaining R7V-1s

had become C-121Js. Another version, still classified, is the TC-121J, a few of which were modified from existing C-121Js.

'Flying Saucer' and 'Hurricane Hunter'

In August 1956 a new version of the WV-2, the WV-2E (later to become the EC-121L) made its first flight; this had the very powerful 'flying saucer' APS-70 radar, which featured a 37ft diameter scanner mounted integrally within a 40ft dish radome on top of an extended dorsal radome which still housed the APS-45 radar of the WV-2, though the ventral AN/APS-20 radar and radome had been removed. This super-structure, which weighed nine tons, had a Vickers hydraulic motor to drive the slowly rotating scanner,

and it was a tribute to the soundness of the Super Connie's triple fins and rudders that such a very big external excrescence could be carried without seriously affecting stability and handling characteristics. Curtailment of US defence spending prevented the WV-2E from going into production, but later the same basic saucer shape was adopted for several other early warning aircraft such as the carrier-based Grumman E-1B Tracer and E-2A Hawkeye. The APS-70 radar in the WV-2E enabled targets to be picked up at three times the range-limit of the WV-2's APS-45 dorsal radar.

With so much of the United States' immunity from attack staked on chains of radar outposts such as DEWline the risk of counter-measures assumed increasing importance, and one manifestation of this concern was the WV-2Q (which later became the EC-121M), a version of the WV-2 specially equipped for electronic countermeasures duties but externally similar to the WV-2. Much of the WV-2Q's work is shrouded in secrecy but it may be assumed that the radar and electronics it carries are progressively up-

This JEC-121K, BuAer 141304, used for missile and satellite tracking from the Pacific Missile Range at Point Mugu, has two additional radar bulges behind the ventral radome and another ahead of the dorsal radome

dated as new countermeasures are developed or new advances in electronics made.

The WV-2 could also be fitted with special equipment for reporting hurricanes and other weather disturbances and in 1955 there appeared the WV-3 (later redesignated WC-121N) 'hurricane hunter', a version of the WV-2 specially equipped for weather reconnaissance and the location and tracking of weather disturbances, in particular hurricanes in the Caribbean area. Special meteorological equipment is carried and a small pressure chamber for releasing radio sonde balloons to measure wind strength and speed is built in. The WV-3 first went into service with

'Hurricane hunter' WC-121N (previously WV-3) BuAer 141323, which started life as a WV-2

Airborne Early Warning Squadron VW-4 at Jacksonville, Florida, in September 1955. The eight WV-3s or WC-121Ns of VW-4 engage in what has been described as the most dangerous sort of flying in the world in tracking the hurricanes that blow up in the Caribbean to strike Florida and other parts of the southern United States. Only the eight WC-121Ns were built and at least one later went to VW-1 squadron.

Two EC-121Ks based at the Naval Air Test Centre at Patuxent River, Maryland, and named *Paisano Dos* and *Kiwi Special* were also used for a series of survey flights to map the Atlantic. The *Kiwi Special* was used on short-range flights and *Paisono Dos* (BuAer 145925) was later specially modified into an NC-121K by Lockheed Aircraft Services for the 'Project Magnet' programme of world-wide oceanic survey initiated by the US Navy Hydrographic Office for the improvement of navigational charts. This involved measuring

Close-up of the forward fuselage of the Project Magnet NC-121K showing the road runner bird and the flags of thirty-two countries visited on oceanic surveys on the nosewheel door

the intensity and direction of the earth's magnetic field (for which a Vector Airborne Magnetometer is fitted) and the study and measurement of cosmic radiation from outer space. To meet the former requirement the rear fuselage had to be demagnetized, magnetic materials being replaced by stainless steel alloys, aluminium and brass, while the electrical circuits had to be rewired and rerouted to eliminate magnetic fields. The dorsal and ventral radomes and all existing radar were removed from *Paisano Dos* and new operational stations and other specialised equipment were installed in the cabin for the normal crew of eighteen Navy personnel and four Project Magnet geophysicists. The Vector Airborne Magnetometer was carried in a detachable streamlined fairing under the fuselage. By late 1964 *Paisano Dos* had flown over 250,000 miles on around-the-world flights, surveying all ocean areas along tracks 200 miles apart.

Ocean Research and Satellite Tracking
Also operating out of Patuxent River is EC-121K, BuAer 145924, named *El Coyote*, which was specially modified into an NC-121K in 1963 by

Lockheed Aircraft Services for research by the Oceanographic Prediction Division of the US Naval Oceanographic Office (NAVOCEANO) into such subjects as thermal structure, sea surface temperatures, ocean waves and low-level meteorological phenomena in ocean areas. Modifications included removal of the dorsal radome and the installation of special scientific equipment, including an infra-red sea surface temperature measuring device, air-launched expendable bathythermographs, wave-height indicators, radiometers, and temperature-pressure-humidity recorders. Operating in conjunction with ocean station vessels, moored buoys and other research ships, *El Coyote* could obtain data from over an area of 100,000 square miles in the course of a single 12-hour flight. Two EC-121Ks are also used by NASA's Goddard Space Flight Centre, while others are employed on missile and satellite tracking from the Pacific missile range at Point Mugu, in California.

Another specially modified Super Constellation was the NC-121D 56-6956 *Triple Nipple*, formerly EC-

Project Magnet NC-121K BuAer 145925 Paisano Dos *specially modified for oceanic surveys with rear fuselage demagnetized and radomes deleted. A Vector Airborne Magnetometer is carried in a streamlined fairing under the fuselage*

121K 143226, converted to carry the Bendix Corporation's TRAP III airborne radiation measurement system. The modification was carried out by the Lockheed Aircraft Services, who delivered this Super Connie to the USAF Aeronautical Systems Division at Wright-Patterson Air Force Base early in 1964. Purpose of the TRAP III aircraft—the acronym signifies Terminal Radiation Airborne Programme—was to scan the skies from a single observation point and obtain visual and precise optical tracking, recording and timing data associated with the re-entry of high-speed bodies, such as space capsules, into the

NC-121K BuAer 145924 El Coyote *specially modified for oceanographic research with the dorsal radome removed*

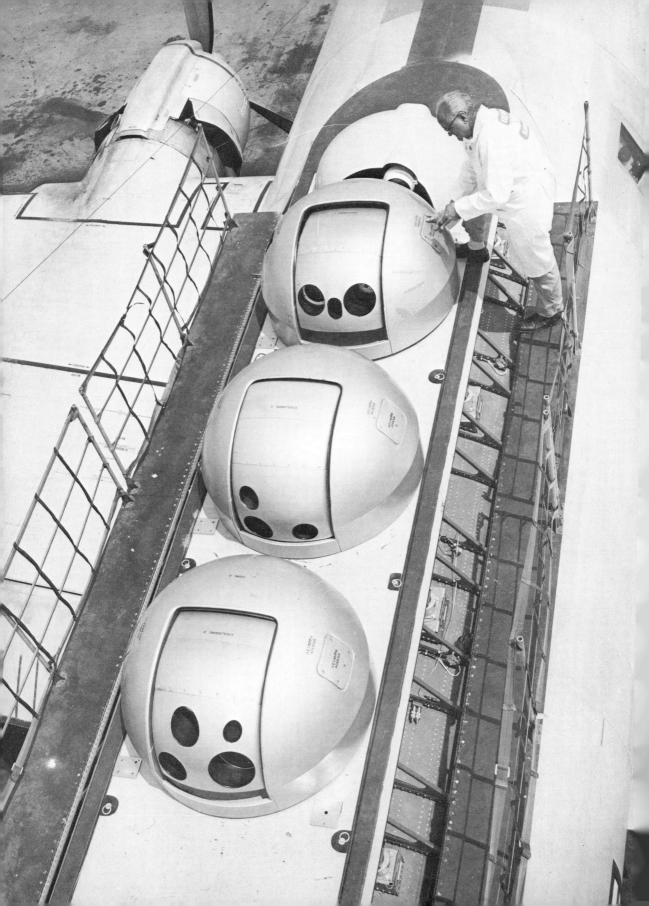

earth's atmosphere. For this both the dorsal and ventral radomes were deleted and a large section of the upper fuselage was removed to make way for three hemispherical domes resembling remotely-controlled gun turrets and containing the optical radiation measurement instrumentation. These domes were mounted on a vibration-isolated rigid platform which could be extended clear of the fuselage for maintenance and with built-in walkways extending on each side for servicing. Both the platform and the domes had to leave the cabin pressurisation and flight characteristics undisturbed; there were also two visual sighting stations provided in the aircraft.

As later types of early warning and maritime patrol aircraft, and more particularly 'spy in the sky' space satellites, came into service the early warning Super Constellation strength was gradually run down in the early 1960s, the 551st and 552nd Airborne Early Warning and Control Wings totalling forty RC-121Ds and EC-121Hs by 1967. A number of new versions have since appeared, some of which are still classified, and these are listed in the Table of Variants.

During the past few years a number of Navy EC-121s have been withdrawn from the Military Aircraft Storage and Disposition Centre for use by the Air Force. EC-121s of the 552nd Wing have been used by the USAF over South Vietnam to direct air strikes against the North from 'safe' air space, and a new role

◄ *NC-121D 56-6956* Tripple Nipple, *formerly EC-121K 143226, takes its name from the hemispherical domes in the top of the fuselage containing optical radiation measurement instruments*

This camouflaged Super Connie with '472' on the nosewheel door is believed to be an EC-121R tactical electronic warfare version. Note the very small USAF 'star and bars' insignia on the fuselage

for this version was brought dramatically to public attention—as well as causing some political consternation—when a US Navy EC-121, engaged on a radar monitoring and electronic eavesdropping flight on behalf of the US National Security Agency, was shot down by North Korean MiG fighters on 15 April 1969 off the Korean coast, about 150 miles south of Vladivostock and well outside the 12-mile territorial waters limit. There were no survivors and only a few pieces of wreckage were retrieved by a Russian search ship.

At the end of 1968 Lockheed fitted an EC-121 with advanced electronic intelligence-gathering equipment as part of the Navy's BLIP (Big Look Improvement Programme), 'Big Look' being the name covering the operations of EC-121s monitoring North Vietnamese surface-to-air missile activity and providing directional information for US aircraft undertaking strikes against radar installations in the North. This EC-121 was fitted with additional sensors, a digital data processor and a more accurate navigational system. Little can be said even now about the latest EC-121 variants, but it is believed that the chief role of the EC-121R version is to monitor Viet Cong troop and vehicle movements along the Ho Chi Minh Trail and in the demilitarised zone between North and South by means of data collected from air-dropped sensors.

A requirement for a new category of aircraft to

replace the Super Constellation and known as AWACS —Airborne Warning and Control System—was evolved by the USAF and in 1970, in the face of strong competition, the main contract went to Boeing for an eight-engined early warning version of the 707-320 carrying a dorsal 'saucer' radome similar in shape to the WV-2E's. Lockheed had produced two earlier proposals for WV-2 developments, the Model CL-257 project, revealed in January 1957, being a new early warning Super Connie with the same 'flying saucer' radome and APS-70 radar as the WV-2E. Five months later Lockheed were awarded a multi-million dollar contract for implementation of the W2V-1, a radar picket derivative of the Model L-1649A Starliner with the latter's new 150 ft span wing and powered by four Allison T-56 turboprops, with two Westinghouse J-34 turbojets in wing-tip pods for cruising at higher altitudes. The disc-shaped dorsal radome of the WV-2E was to have been featured, but with twin fins and rudders, and the maximum gross weight was to have been about 175,000lb. First flight was scheduled for late 1959 or early 1960 but only a month after the contract award had been announced, a defence budget squeeze obliged the US Navy to abandon the project and the pre-production engineering phase of the W2V-1 was cancelled, though the Phase 1 portion of the contract, covering design studies, wind-tunnel tests and the fuselage mock-up, was continued for a time.

8: The Super G

Perhaps no other single factor can influence the development of a successful aeroplane as much as its engines, and the Constellation was yet another example of a type where successive weight and payload increases were made possible by the engine manufacturers coming up with more power at just the right moment. With the Model L-1049E, Lockheed had gone about as far as it could in raising the weight without additional power but the Wright company came forward with a new version of the Turbo-Compound, the 3,250bhp (maximum take-off) R-3350-972TC18 DA-3, to power the next version, the Model L-1049G Super Constellation, or Super G as it was also called. The 'DA-3 Turbo-Compound incorporated oil system changes, superchargers with improved impellers and shell-cast diffusers for improved critical altitude performance, and an increase in METO power from 2,600bhp to 2,700bhp in low blower at 2,600rpm. This enabled the Model L-1049G's maximum gross weight to be raised to 137,500lb and the landing weight to 113,000lb; the maximum zero fuel weight was initially 103,500lb but was increased to 108,000lb from early in 1956, thus allowing more payload to be carried and greater flexibility in the choice of payload/range combinations over different routes. This zero fuel weight increase was primarily useful to those airlines which needed a combination passenger/cargo interior with freight carried in the forward part of the cabin, and also came in useful when L-1049Gs, displaced as first-line equipment by the big jets, came to be converted into freighters.

The Super G also featured as an optional 'extra' the 600 US gal wing-tip tanks fitted on the early warning WV-2s and RC-121s, and several Model L-1049E operators, including KLM, Iberia, Avianca and Air–India, had their aircraft modified to 1049G standard with these tanks, while Trans-Canada had two of its 1049E-55s so modified but without the tip tanks. Maximum range of the Super G with these tanks was 4,620 miles with reserves and the absolute range was 5,840 miles; fuel capacity was increased from 6,550 US gal to 7,750 US gal. Weather radar, either the RCA AVQ-10 or Bendix RDR-7 sets, could also be fitted, and it increased the fuselage length by 34in to 116ft 2in. A chordwise type Goodrich de-icer boot installation for the wings and tail was featured. The cabin soundproofing was improved by blankets of a new fibreglass material attached to the inner surface of the cabin skin, an inner wall made of sound-insulating plyboard was introduced, and rubber shock pads on the engine mounts helped to isolate the cabin from noise and vibration. The same range of Henry Dreyfuss-styled interiors as on the L-1049C and L-1049E was available for the Super G, which could seat up to ninety-nine passengers and six crew, and the cabin length was 92ft.

Altogether the Super G embodied 107 design improvements over the 1049E and the first example, for Northwest Orient Airlines, which had originally ordered six on 20 April 1953 (the order was later reduced to four), was rolled out in late November 1954. It first flew on 17 December of that year, and the first delivery to Northwest was on 22 January 1955. The airline put its Super Gs on to the 'Great Circle' routes from the US west coast to the Far East, linking Seattle and Tacoma to Tokyo, Okinawa and Manila via Anchorage (Alaska) and also operating first/tourist-class flights between Seattle/Tacoma and Honolulu via Portland, supplementing the DC-6B tourist flights over this route. Later, DC-6Bs took over all the Honolulu services and the Super Gs operated a service between Tokyo and Seoul (Korea). When Northwest decided as a matter of policy to reduce the multiplicity of types in its fleet—comprising all four major types of piston-engined airliner, the Super Constellation, the DC-6B, the Boeing Stratocruiser and the DC-7C, as well as the smaller DC-4—the four Super Gs, after only two years' service with Northwest, were sold, in 1957, to Linea Aeropostal Venezolana. There they supplemented the two 1049Es and a 1049G already in service, and a sixth Super G, YV-C-AMI, was later acquired. Northwest's 1049Gs accommodated between

*First to take delivery of the 1049G was Northwest
Orient, which used its four on routes to Tokyo,
Okinawa, Manila and Honolulu. N5172V
seen here was sold to LAV as YV-C-ANB*

fifty and seventy-four passengers in first/tourist
interiors divided up into five main compartments, one
of which could be used for freight carrying if desired.

Altogether 104 Super Gs were to be built and the next
customer to take delivery after Northwest was TWA,
which ordered twelve on 22 October 1953 and eight
more in November 1955. These were fitted with both
tip tanks and weather radar, trials of the latter being
made on three aircraft before equipping the whole

*TWA ordered a fleet of twenty-eight 1049Gs and
put this version into service between New York and
Los Angeles on 1 April 1955 and on the Washington–
London route on 1 November of that year*

fleet. General Electric two-compartment air circulation
ovens enabling sixty meals of pre-cooked frozen food
to be prepared simultaneously were featured, and no
less than 700lb of soundproofing was fitted to quieten
the cabin. Initially, there was accommodation for
sixty-six passengers in three compartments, plus an
eight-berth sleeper section and a four-seat lounge, but
for the North Atlantic routes the seating was reduced
to forty-nine passengers. TWA inaugurated Super
G services over the New York–Los Angeles route on
1 April 1955 and put it into service over the Atlantic
on its Washington–London route on 1 November
1955, having been forestalled by Lufthansa as the first
transatlantic operator of the 1049G. By the spring of
1956 TWA Super G schedules across the Atlantic had
built up to fifty crossings a week in a concentrated effort
to wrest traffic away from Pan American's Strato-

cruiser and DC-6B services. Pan Am had introduced the DC-7B on 13 June 1955 and the DC-7C on 1 June 1956, the latter giving it a lead which TWA was not to equal until a year later when it introduced the Model L-1649A Starliner.

Other Super G Operators

A number of other transatlantic operators followed TWA in ordering the Super G to supplement earlier 1049 models on their Atlantic and other routes. Trans-Canada Airlines ordered two Model L-1049G-82s in 1955 and two more in December 1956, while KLM ordered four 1049Gs in 1954 besides taking delivery in June and July 1956 of two ordered by Thai Airways Co and sold by the latter to the Dutch airline before delivery. Air France ordered 14 L-1049Gs in three batches, the first early in 1954, and these featured the tip tanks but not weather radar; the interiors could be converted in three hours from the 32-seat 'The Golden Parisian' layout to an 81-seater tourist interior, while twenty-four first-class and thirty-four tourist passengers could be carried in a two-class arrangement. One was later converted into a freighter similar to the Model L-1049C freighter conversions and another was leased to Tunis Air, in which Air France had a 49 per cent interest, in 1961. Air France 1049Gs operated a Phnom Penh–Hong Kong route for the Cambodian airline, Royal Air Cambodge, from 11 February 1959 until replaced by 707s in January 1961. Air France Super Constellations also operated a service at sub-economy-type T2-class fares (later a first-class and economy service) for Royal Air Maroc from Oujda in Morocco to Toulouse and Paris to supplement the latter's Caravelle services over similar routes.

The Spanish airline, Iberia, ordered two 1049Gs in December 1955 with tip tanks and weather radar, these accommodating a crew of eleven and sixty-three passengers. In addition, two of the ex-Thai Airways Super Gs were leased by KLM to Iberia in 1961 and subsequently sold to them on 15 August 1962. Iberia also acquired a third ex-Thai Airways Super G that had been sold to Guest Aerovias Mexico SA by SAS and later leased to Aerovias Panama Airways. Iberia, in turn, leased its 1049Gs to the Spanish independent Aviaco, in which it has a major shareholding, for the inclusive tour holiday charter traffic.

Avianca of Colombia took delivery of a 1049G in October 1955 to supplement its three 1049Es on its routes to Europe and New York, and this was later operated with an 84-passenger layout. Cubana had ordered a Model L-1049E to supplement its older ex-Pan Am Model L-049Es, and this was delivered on 22 November 1954, setting up a Los Angeles–Havana record of 7hr 20min on its 2,300 miles delivery flight. Fitted out to seat seventy-four passengers, this 1049E was immediately put on to the Havana–Madrid route via Bermuda, Santa Maria in the Azores and Lisbon, and also operated the Havana–Mexico City and Havana–New York routes. It was sold to Seaboard & Western after less than two years with Cubana and in its place the first of three Super Gs was delivered on 20 February 1956, 1049G services over the Havana–Madrid route

Two of Air-India's 1049Gs, VT-DJW Rani of Bijapur and VT-DJX Rani of Sagurai, were converted into freighters by Lockheed Aircraft Services

beginning on 14 March 1956. Cubana's Super Gs had tip tanks and RCA AVQ-10 weather radar. With Fidel Castro's accession to power in 1959, and Cuba's alignment with the Communist bloc, the services to Miami and New York were abandoned in 1961 and a Havana–Prague Britannia service was substituted for the traditional Atlantic route to Madrid. Russian types such as the Ilyushin Il-18 and Il-14 replaced the Viscount turboprops, which were sold off, and the Super Constellations, which were withdrawn from use.

Eastern Air Lines ordered ten L-1049Gs in September 1955, and these were fitted with a 'Golden Falcon' interior and four-abreast seating for 70–88 passengers; later, from 1962, a 95-passenger layout

The two Qantas 1049Gs VH-EAO Southern Aurora *and VH-EAP* Southern Zephyr *before departure from Sydney Airport on 14 January 1958 on the first round-the-world service. VH-EAO, under the command of Capt M. Bamman, flew across the Pacific to San Francisco, New York and London and VH-EAP, flown by Capt R. J. Davis, took the 'Kangaroo' route through Singapore to London. Both aircraft arrived back in Sydney on 20 January, having circumnavigated the globe in opposite directions*

for the 'Air Shuttle' services was introduced, with a flight crew and cabin staff of five. For these flights extra windows were fitted aft of the main entrance door. Eastern's ten Super Gs were re-engined from 1956 with 3,400bhp (maximum take-off) limited to 3,250 bhp R-3350-988TC18EA-3 Turbo-Compounds, this being almost the same engine variant as powered the Model L-1649A Starliner. These later powerplants were installed for greater engine durability and easier maintenance rather than more power.

Air-India ordered three Super Gs in September 1955 and two later to supplement its 1049Cs and 1049Es. The two latter ones were later converted into freighters (with alternative passenger-carrying layouts) by Lockheed Aircraft Services after they had been displaced as first-line equipment by the Boeing 707 in 1960. With the rest of their Constellation fleet, Air-India's four remaining Super Gs (one had crashed on 19 July 1959) were sold off to the Indian Air Force in 1962. Qantas took delivery of the first of two L-1049G-82-118s on 20 October 1955, these being the two whose delivery positions were released when Northwest Orient cut back its Super G order from six to four. Two

more were ordered in the autumn of 1956, and one was used to test the Loran long-range navigational aid in 1958. Model L-1049G VH-EAO *Southern Aurora* was sold to Lockheed in 1959 as N9722C but was leased back in 1960 to replace the first 1049G, which had been lost in an accident at Mauritius on 25 August 1960; for this lease it was appropriately renamed *Southern Prodigal*.

Apart from Air–India, there was another Asian carrier, Thai Airways, which twice ordered L-1049G

Thai Airways ordered three 1049Gs but they were sold by SAS; HS-TCC seen here became XA-NAE of Guest, and later EC-ARN Santiago of Iberia

TAP of Portugal bought two of the ex-Thai 1049Gs, CS-TLE having been XA-NAD of Guest and HS-TCB

Super Constellations but was never able to start international operations with them. The first two were ordered in the summer of 1953 and, as related previously, were sold to KLM before delivery, this move being made to ease the airline's financial commitments. Three years later three Super Gs were ordered after the US International Co-operation Administration had given a $2 million grant to the airline and Pan American had started to provide technical and operational assistance. The Super Gs were delivered from July 1957 but remained lying idle at Bangkok for some months while the airline's international competitive position deteriorated in spite of the US ICA grant and Pan Am's assistance. Eventually, in 1960, the three aircraft were sold to Guest Aerovias Mexico SA (previously Aerovias Guest). Guest had operated Model L-749 services to Miami and Madrid, and the Super Gs replaced three ex-SAS DC-6s which had reopened the Mexico City–Madrid route in 1959 via Miami, Bermuda, Santa Maria in the Azores and Lisbon, with the addition of Paris as the European terminal. When Guest was reorganised in 1961 the three Super Gs were sold (after two had been leased for a short time to Aerovias Panama Airways), one to Iberia and two to Transportes Aéreos Portugueses SARL (TAP). These supplemented the three L-1049G-82s ordered by the Portuguese airline in December 1953 and delivered in July and September

1955, complete with weather radar. TAP's Super Gs operated services from Lisbon to Luanda (Angola) and Lourenco Marques (Mozambique) via Kano (Nigeria) and Leopoldville, and were also deployed on the more important European routes such as Lisbon–London, as well as operating the Lisbon–Oporto domestic route for a time.

Another new Super G operator was the Brazilian airline Varig—SA Emprêsa de Viação Aérea Rio Grandense—named after its home state of Rio Grande do Sul where it was founded in 1927. It had ordered three Super Gs in April 1953 and on 2 August 1955 a Varig 1049G inaugurated a new route from Rio to New York via Belem, Port of Spain (Trinidad) and Cuidad Trujillo (Dominican Republic). Since Varig already operated into Montevideo and Buenos Aires, it could now offer through-plane service from the Argentine capital all the way to New York, and the initial weekly frequency was increased to thrice-weekly in 1956. The new service to New York soon became popular and Varig began to make serious traffic inroads into the mighty Pan American, no mean feat for a relative newcomer to the international scene. Varig's Super Gs were displaced as first-line equipment by 707s in 1960 and were put on to the major domestic and regional routes.

Varig's Super Gs had Bendix weather radar and accommodation for fifty-nine passengers. In June 1956 the airline ordered two Model L-1649A Starliners for delivery beginning in December 1957 but in the spring of 1957 this order was changed to a repeat one for three more Super Gs as Varig preferred to standardise on this

Varig originally ordered two Model 1649As but changed this to a repeat order for three 1049Gs one of which, PP-VDE, is seen here at Rio's Galeao airport

version. Varig's five Super Gs (one had been lost in an accident on 16 August 1957) and four ex-REAL L-1049Hs were withdrawn from service in the summer of 1966, by which time they were no longer airworthy. (Varig had acquired the REAL Aerovias Nacional airline group in August 1961.)

Perhaps the best-known of all the new operators who started with the Super G Constellation was the re-born Deutsche Lufthansa AG, the bearer of a famous name in air transport dating back to 1926. Four Model L-1049Gs had been ordered late in 1953 by its predecessor, Luftag, a provisional stock company, and the first of these was delivered on 29 March, 1955. A New York service from Hamburg, Dusseldorf or Frankfurt via Shannon and Gander (technical stop) was inaugurated on 8 June of that year and, in the following April, the 'Manchester Mid-Western' service linking

Lufthansa ordered eight 1049Gs in two batches of four to resume post-war international operations over long-haul routes; D-ALAP seen here was the first of the second batch

Manchester direct to Chicago. Paris and Montreal were later added to the Atlantic route. On 15 August 1956 Lufthansa returned to an old sphere of influence with the introduction of a service to Rio and Buenos Aires (with Montevideo and Santiago added later) and in September extended their network to the Middle East, a second batch of four Super Gs, ordered in 1955, having now been delivered. On 1 November 1959, the Super Gs inaugurated a Far East route to Bangkok

Air Ceylon leased KLM 1049E with tip-tanks, PH-LKA Isotoop, *which later became 4R-ACH* Soma Devi

through Cairo, Karachi and Calcutta. They were superseded by Boeing 707s on the New York services from March 1960 and on the Far East route in January 1961, and were thereafter progressively replaced on the trunk routes they had initiated.

All eight of the Lufthansa Super Gs had tip tanks but not weather radar, and originally, in 1956, seated sixteen first-class passengers in 'slumberette'-type seats in two rear compartments and forty-nine tourist-class passengers. A 40-passenger first-class interior for the South American route was introduced, as well as a de luxe 32-seat interior for the twice-weekly 'The Senator' service to the USA. The latter was aimed at the business traffic over the Atlantic, and proved so successful that Lufthansa made 'The Senator' its new standard first-class service on its South American and Far East routes. Lufthansa installed the furnishings, seats and fittings, including the complete galleys, in their Super Gs at Hamburg as they were delivered from Lockheed, and initially, while German crews were being trained, the Super Gs were flown by TWA captains with Lockheed flight engineers and navigators from the US 'non-sked' Transocean Airlines.

Lufthansa's Super Gs all had the first-class accommodation removed from April 1963, for operation in an all-economy layout, and several were converted to seat eighty-six passengers for the thrice-daily Hamburg–Frankfurt 'walk-on' air bus service inaugurated on 1 April of that year. The seven remaining Super Gs (one had been lost in an accident at Rio on 11 January 1959) were grounded in the late summer of 1962 for modifications following the discovery of a fatigue crack in the front spar of one aircraft near the inboard engine nacelle, and were out of service for a few weeks. From late in 1962, the Super Gs were fitted with Mallite EGB (end-grain balsa) laminated flooring in certain areas. One Super G was leased to Seaboard & Western for a time in 1958 and others to Alitalia in 1962 and 1963 for the latter's Milan–Rimini flights. All seven were finally withdrawn from service in 1968.

9: The Model L-1049H

On 29 June 1955 Lockheed announced the Model L-1049H, a freighter version of the Super G with the same freight doors and heavy-duty, anti-corrosion magnesium floor of the Model L-1049D. In a matter of hours, it could be converted to a high-density passenger layout by the addition of such things as vinyl interior walls, baggage racks, curtains, reading lights, toilets and a buffet. Up to 118 passengers could be carried, or 104 at a seat pitch of 38in with a crew of up to eleven, passenger seats being stowed in the under-floor freight holds when the cabin was converted back to freight. A maximum gross weight of 137,500lb was originally achieved, the same as the Super G's, but this was increased to 140,000lb when the L-1049H went into service with the 'EA-6 Turbo-Compounds giving more cruising power. Instead of the 'DA-3 Turbo-Compounds of the Super G, the L-1049H was usually powered by 3,400bhp (maximum take-off) limited to 3,250bhp R-3350-988TC18 EA-3 Turbo-Compounds giving easier maintenance and greater durability; Eastern had had its Super Gs re-engined with this R-3350 variant. Tip tanks, as on the Super G, could be fitted and the Model L-1049H's fuel capacity was the same, giving it a range of 4,313 miles with three hours' fuel reserves as a passenger aircraft, or 3,393 miles as a freighter; a payload of up to 19 short tons could be carried on the North Atlantic routes. A payload of 40,203lb of freight could be carried at the 137,500lb gross weight under the 5 per cent overload conditions authorised by the Civil Aeronautics Administration, but a more normal payload was 35,118lb. The freight hold volume and cargo door dimensions were the same as on the Model L-1049D, but the L-1049H, unlike the earlier version, retained the same number of cabin windows as the Super G besides having a smaller passenger door inset into the upward-opening rear cargo door. The hold dimensions could accommodate such loads as a 73ft length of 10in pipe, or a package measuring 3ft 6in wide × 5ft high × 20ft long.

The first customer for the new version, of which fifty-three were to be built, was Qantas, which ordered two Model L-1049H-82-133s, the first of these, VH-EAM *Southern Spray*, making its first flight on 20 September 1956. In addition, Qantas had two of its L-1049E/01-55s converted into freighters in 1960, and with these and the 1049Hs an all-freight service from Sydney to London was operated. The Qantas order

The convertible passenger/freighter Model 1049H was widely used by major US supplemental carriers like Capitol, which acquired this one from Seaboard

*Seaboard 1049E N1005C was leased to Inter-
continental US Inc in 1962, and later to TAP,
Capitol and Aerlinte Eireann*

was followed by one from Seaboard & Western
Airlines for two, plus three more ordered at the end of
1955. In addition, Seaboard had bought a Model
L-1049E from Cubana and in 1958 had leased a Super
G from Lufthansa, besides having two of its Model
L-1049Ds modified up to Model L-1049H/03 standard
in the summer of 1956 with a higher gross weight of
135,400lb, later increased to 137,500lb. Seaboard used

*Jim Flannery's Constellation Lounge and Restaurant,
alias Model 1049E N1005C, purchased from Capitol
in August 1967. It was dismantled at Newcastle airport,
Delaware, and re-erected at Penndel, Penn, on Route 1
on 25-ft high aerofoil-shaped concrete supports. There
is seating for seventy-two people in airline-type seats
and a cocktail bar*

its 1049Hs not only for its scheduled cargo services
across the Atlantic to cities in Europe and for civil and
military charters, but also leased them out extensively
to other operators to whom the L-1049H's quick convertibility to passenger-carrying was especially valuable. An early example was the lease of 1049Hs to
Eastern at the end of 1956 to cater for the extra
Christmas holiday traffic on the routes from New York
and other cities to Miami, and early in 1958 the
Belgian airline, Sabena, leased three 1049Hs for the
duration of the Brussels Exhibition. The ex-Cubana
L-1049E was leased to the US 'non-sked', Intercontinental Airways, or Intercontinental US Inc, in
1962, which was engaged in world-wide charters in
association with the Luxembourg charter carrier,
Interocean Airways. Transtate Airlines, a subsidiary
of Intercontinental, applied in November 1963 to
operate a New York–Buffalo 'walk-on' service with

84-passenger L-1049Hs but permission was not granted by the CAB. The L-1049E was later leased to TAP of Portugal (which also leased a Seaboard L-1049H during 1958–59) and to Capitol Airways (on 1 June 1965) as well as to Aerlinte Eireann. An L-1049H was also leased to Intercontinental by Seaboard, and later to Transtate, and the former also used a second L-1049H.

Seaboard's best-known leasing operation was the provision of two L-1049Hs (plus the L-1049E) and flight crews on a mileage basis to the Irish airline, Aerlinte Eireann, which had taken delivery of five L-749s in 1947 to begin a service to New York but had sold the aircraft to BOAC after a change of government had caused a deferment of these plans. A new agreement with Seaboard in November 1952 to provide aircraft for an Atlantic service beginning in 1953 also proved abortive when the CAB declined to give approval for more than a two-year period and Aerlinte's third and successful attempt was timed to coincide with the introduction of IATA economy-class fares over the Atlantic. The Seaboard agreement of 1952 was revised and updated, and on 28 April 1958 a thrice-weekly Dublin–Shannon–New York service was inaugurated with the L-1049Hs fitted out to seat ninety-five passengers. In June, the frequency was stepped up to seven flights a week, reducing during the winter months, and a stop at Boston was added in October 1958. The L-1049Hs continued this service until, with the introduction by the Irish airline of Boeing 720-048 jet service on 14 December 1960, the lease was terminated. Aerlinte also used the Super G which Seaboard leased from Lufthansa. In the summer of 1962 Seaboard leased seven of its Super Constellations (three L-1049Ds and four L-1049Hs) to Capitol Airways, which, exercising an option to purchase, eventually bought two L-1049Ds and an L-1049H.

Slick Airways, another US scheduled freight service operator, had ordered five L-1049Hs at about the same time as Seaboard but later postponed this order when mounting losses on its transcontinental freight routes forced it to suspend all scheduled services on 22 February 1958. However, it continued military charter flying and the leasing of aircraft, and finally acquired three L-1049Hs from Lockheed ex-storage in 1959, plus two more operated by the Argentine airline Transcontinental SA. Slick resumed scheduled freight services in April 1962, and also operated L-1049H flights across the Pacific under various charter contracts for the USAF Military Air Transport Service. It had three more ex-California Eastern Aviation L-1049Hs on lease from World Airways from September 1963 until the end of 1965, but in July of the following year Slick's financial difficulties became acute and its fleet, including the L-1049Hs plus an ex-Alaska Airlines one, were acquired by Airlift International of Miami (formerly Riddle Airlines), which later sold one of the L-1049Hs to Bal Trade. Slick had also used an ex-Trans-Canada 1049 for a time, and its 1049Hs were later fitted with the 3,440bhp (maximum take-off) R-3350-988TC18 EA-6 Turbo-Compounds

Slick Airways used its 1049Hs, including N6937C seen here, on its US transcontinental freight routes and flights across the Pacific under MATS contract

giving 150hp greater cruising power, (1,975hp in low blower).

The US 'non-sked', California Eastern Aviation, had ordered three L-1049Hs in the spring of 1956, these being originally intended for the newly-started Argentine airline, Transcontinental SA, in which California Eastern had a financial interest, as well as providing technical and operational assistance. The three L-1049Hs were leased to the Hughes Tool Co at

the beginning of 1958 for use by TWA for three years at a monthly rental of $45,000 per aircraft, and with these TWA inaugurated a twice-weekly London–New York all-cargo service on 6 October 1959. The California Eastern aircraft were returned in January 1961 and later sold to World Airways. Hughes Tool also leased for TWA's use from February 1958 the two L-1049Hs ordered by Resort Airlines in the spring of 1956 for military contract cargo operations and for inclusive tour traffic, Resort being one of the first US carriers to specialise in the latter type of business. Resort provided packaged holiday tours to the Caribbean and its L-1049Hs were fitted out to seat ninety-six passengers. One was lost in an accident on 24 November 1959 and the other was leased to World Airways just before Resort ceased operations on 1 July 1961. In addition to its leased L-1049Hs, Hughes Tool also ordered four new L-1049Hs for

TWA's use, these being sold to Trans-International Airlines in September 1961.

To return to the Argentine operator, Transcontinental SA, two 1049Hs were employed by this airline to inaugurate a Buenos Aires–New York service via Sao Paulo, Rio de Janeiro and Caracas in September 1958. On replacement by two Britannia 308 turboprops in March 1960, the two 1049Hs were acquired by Slick.

Another South American airline, REAL Aerovias Nacional of Brazil (the initials stood for Rêdes Estaduais Aéreas Ltda) ordered four 1049Hs in May 1957. These had accommodation for eighty-one passengers but could be adapted to a luxury first-class interior, and tip tanks were fitted. Established in 1946 REAL, by a series of mergers of and acquisitions in fourteen other Brazilian airlines, had become the largest airline in South America, serving over 200

Resort Airlines took delivery of two 1049Hs in 1957, N101R and N102R; the latter, seen here, was lost in an accident

places in Brazil. The L-1049Hs went into service on routes from Sao Paulo and Rio to Miami and Los Angeles, but perhaps the most interesting of the airline's L-1049H routes was an extension in May 1960 of the Los Angeles service to Tokyo via Honolulu and Wake Island, with an eye to the many immigrants of Japanese origin who had made their homes in Brazil. This was the first direct air service between Brazil and Japan, but it had to be suspended when, in May 1961,

REAL Aerovias Nacional used its four 1049Hs on routes from Brazil to Miami and Los Angeles, and also to Tokyo via Wake Island and Honolulu

Varig purchased a majority holding in Aerovias Brazil, the international division of REAL, later acquiring a controlling interest in the whole REAL Aerovias Nacional airline group. The L-1049Hs then passed into Varig service and were finally withdrawn from use in the summer of 1966.

Another L-1049H customer to use the type in the passenger rôle was National Airlines of Miami, which ordered four late in 1956. Fitted out to seat 109 passengers, and carrying weather radar and tip tanks, they were used on National's routes from the Eastern seaboard cities to Florida and also operated a New York–Miami all-freight service. They were finally retired early in 1962 and sold off late in 1964 to Nordair of Montreal, which used them to operate charters across the Atlantic and to Jamaica; an L-1049H was leased to Eastern Provincial Airways in 1969.

KLM also used its L-1049Hs, three of which it had ordered in 1957, for passenger services, with seating accommodation for 101, later diverting them to all-freight services. Two more L-1049Hs ordered by Trans-Canada Airlines were again used mainly for passenger-carrying, and one, CF-TEZ, was involved in an overshoot accident and rebuilt in 1962 using parts of L-1049C-55, CF-TGC, after which it was sold to California Airmotive as N9640Z. The surviving 1049H was sold to Trans-International Airlines through Lockheed in May 1961. Pakistan International

Pakistan International ordered two 1049Hs, AP-AJY (below) and AP-AJZ, for all-freight and passenger services on its 'inter-wing' flights between East and West Pakistan

Airlines ordered two 1049Hs in mid-1957 to supplement its three L-1049Cs and used them both for all-freight and tourist-class flights on the 'inter-wing' services linking Karachi and Lahore in West Pakistan to Dacca in East Pakistan, now Bangladesh.

Transocean Airlines, one of the biggest US 'non-skeds' or supplemental carriers, took delivery of the first of its two L-1049Hs in the summer of 1957 on lease from the Air Finance Corporation, a company formed by Conrad and Barron Hilton of the Hilton Hotels Corporation and Joseph Drown, an independent hotel owner, to buy airliners and lease them to airlines preferring rental to an outright purchase commitment. Transocean used its L-1049Hs, fitted out to seat ninety-two passengers, on a once-weekly, low-fare trans-Pacific service from Oakland, California to Okinawa via Honolulu, Wake Island and Guam, which was largely patronised by personnel at the US military base on Okinawa. Later, a Transocean L-1049H was leased to Lufthansa for the latter's Frankfurt–New York all-freight service, and an order for four more was cancelled when Transocean went out of business in the summer of 1960. Another financing company in the airline field was the Standard Factors Corporation of New York, which ordered two L-1049Hs late in 1956 for lease to airlines, with an option to purchase.

The largest L-1049H operator was the Flying Tiger Line, which ordered ten in September 1955, plus five later. In addition, the company leased an L-1049A from TWA for a time in 1960, an ex-Resort Airlines L-1049H from World Airways in 1964, and two ex-KLM L-1049Hs from World in July 1963, which they eventually bought in April 1966. They also acquired

an ex-Qantas L-1049E/01-55 which they sold to the charter operator, Atlantic Airways of Miami, in 1969, while the 1049A leased from TWA in 1960 later went to Paramount Airlines. Altogether Fying Tiger operated twenty-three Super Constellations bought outright or on lease, by far the largest fleet of these aircraft to be used for freighting.

Flying Tiger used its Super Connies for scheduled all-freight services across the States over a route linking Boston, Hartford/Springfield and New York to Chicago, Los Angeles and San Francisco, also calling at Binghampton, Philadelphia, Cleveland, Detroit and Minneapolis/St Paul, with connecting services from San Francisco to Portland and Seattle, this being known as US Airfreight Route No 100. In addition, a good deal of contract charter flying was done, the L-1049Hs flying for the MATS across the Pacific from San Francisco to Tokyo, Okinawa and Manila via Wake Island and Honolulu, and across the Atlantic carrying Jamaican emigrants to Britain, student groups, convention delegates and numerous other group charters. As many as 120 passengers have been carried at a time in an L-1049H flight, although a more typical interior seated 99-114 passengers for the trans-Pacific flights and 118 for trans-Atlantic charters; the interiors were quickly convertible for freighting and featured General Electric galley equipment.

The 'EA-3 Turbo-Compounds that powered Flying Tiger's 1049Hs were converted to the 'EA-6 versions after delivery to give 150hp greater cruising power, and the original solid dural airscrews were replaced by Hamilton Standard hollow-bladed airscrews which saved 600lb weight on each aircraft. The 'EA-6 Turbo-

Largest operator of the 1049H was the Flying Tiger Line, which used them for US transcontinental freight services and charter flights. N6923C is seen here

Compounds enabled the maximum gross weight to be raised from the original 137,500lb to 140,000lb, the higher gross weight adding about 300 miles more range on US domestic flights by allowing 2,500lb more fuel to be carried, and payload to be increased from 37,000lb to 39,500lb on overwater flights such as San Francisco-Honolulu. The first L-1049H approved for the higher gross weight was delivered to Flying Tiger in the spring of 1957, and on 11 March of that year an L-1049H carried a record commercial air freight load of 41,746lb of general cargo from Newark (New Jersey) to Burbank.

An L-1049H was leased to Lufthansa in 1960, and two more to Trans-International Airlines on 14 November of that year by Lockheed, one being bought by TIA on 1 March 1964, but both were repurchased by Flying Tiger on 30 September 1966. L-1049H N6919C was leased to Korean Airlines on 14 April 1966 as HL-4002, this operator having previously leased a Model L-749A from Transocean for the Seoul-Hong Kong route, which was discontinued in 1963. The L-1049H was used by Korean mainly for charter work and was returned to Flying Tiger on 4 December 1967.

Second-Hand Super G and H Sales
Like the earlier Super Constellations, the Models L-1049G and L-1049H found ready buyers in the second-hand airliner market but as the 1960s pro-

Trans-International was another US supplemental which operated a fleet mix of 1049Gs and 1049Hs; 1049G N9751C seen here was previously N9721C and VH-EAD Southern Dew of Qantas

gressed jets became more and more essential for the best charter business and so it was that the later Super Connie variants achieved the greatest prominence (and some notoriety) in operations such as the Biafra airlift. Capitol Airways had one of the biggest used Super Connie fleets and acquired its first L-1049G in January 1960. This had been built for Howard Hughes and delivered as long ago as 24 February 1956 but, like most airliners built to the personal order of Hughes, it had done little flying for him and when it was returned to Lockheed, Capitol traded in one of their L-749As in part exchange for it. An ex-Transocean L-1049H was bought from the Babb Co, the parent company of Transocean, in April 1959, and two more ex-Seaboard World L-1049Hs several years later. The four ex-Hughes Tool (for TWA) L-1049Hs sold to Trans-International Airlines were leased by them to Capitol in 1962–63, and Capitol also purchased an ex-Qantas L-1049G that had been sold back to Lockheed in March 1960; this Super G later went to Trans-International and to Standard Airways.

The last of Capitol's Super Connies was phased out early in 1968 when replaced by Douglas DC-8 jets and the remaining twelve L-1049s in Capitol service, plus an L-749A, were put up for disposal at Wilmington;

altogether Capitol had operated seventeen L-1049s and L-749s since 1955. One of the last charter jobs to be undertaken by Capitol's L-1049s was a series of inclusive tour flights out of Berlin on behalf of the Berliner Flug Ring travel agency, three or four of these aircraft being based on Berlin for this purpose.

American Flyers Airline Corp acquired the Qantas Super G VH-EAO *Southern Prodigal* on lease from California Airmotive as N86682, as well as two more L-1049s from other sources, while another ex-Qantas Super G went to Resort Airlines in 1959 to supplement the two L-1049Hs it had ordered. In 1968 a new charter operator, called Air Mid-East, was formed with a single Super Constellation and by 1970 claimed to have built up its fleet to eight 115-passenger L-1049s from various sources, six DC-7s and four DC-6s. It intended to specialise in charters throughout the Middle East but very little has been heard of it in recent years. Another little-known L-1049 operator was Rutas Aereas Panamenas SA which was operating an ex-Thai Airways and Guest 1049G, HP-467, for Cia Interamericana Export-Import SA. The latter had it on lease from the used-aircraft dealers International Aerodyne of Miami when it crashed just after taking off from Panama City on a freight flight on 30 March 1968, killing the crew of three. The export-import company for whom it was being operated also acquired a second Super Connie, an ex-Iberia L-1049E, from International Aerodyne.

One of Trans-Canada's surplus Super Gs was later

involved in a gun-running episode; this was CF-TEX, sold to Douglas as N9642Z and later to California Airmotive. It was leased to Continental Councellors and then, from early 1965, went on lease-purchase to Walter Vonderahe of Van Nuys who lease-purchased it to a charter operator called United States Airways. The aircraft had already been in trouble at Gatwick on 22 January 1965 when it was detained for failing to take a charter party of West Indians to Jamaica, but on 2 February it was allowed to leave for Amsterdam, ostensibly on a charter for Trans-Africa Aircoach. It landed at Beek in southern Holland where, after the bogus Ghanaian 'registration' 9G-28 had been painted on the fuselage and false papers provided, it left for Prague to carry a cargo of illegal arms to the Congo. Engine trouble forced it to land at Luqa, Malta, where most of the arms on board were confiscated and the three-man crew fined £300. The aircraft was not released until 29 January 1966 and was then re-possessed by Mr Vonderahe, who had received only one instalment of $10,000 as down payment on the aircraft from US Airways; the bogus 'registration' N964 was also applied.

A far more substantial operator was one of the major US supplementals, World Airways, which leased three L-1049Hs from California Eastern Aviation in January 1961, a fourth, ex-Transocean one, N1880 from the 1880 Corp in the same month, and an ex-Resort L-1049H on 3 May 1961, plus two more leased from KLM in 1962. The ex-California Eastern aircraft went to Slick from September 1963 and later to Airlift International, and the ex-Resort and KLM L-1049Hs went to Flying Tiger, while the ex-Transocean

L-1049H later went to Alaska Airlines on lease in May 1964, and then to Montreal Air Services and Airlift International. Alaska also acquired a second ex-Qantas L-1049H on lease late in 1962.

In the Far East, Air America, which operates a sizeable fleet of small aircraft on quasi-military operations in Laos against the Communist Pathet Lao (Free Laos) guerillas, acquired an L-1049H from Flying Tiger late in 1963 for linking its base at Tainan (Taiwan) to other parts of the Far East. And another ex-Flying Tiger L-1049H was acquired by China Airlines, now the national airline of Formosa or Taiwan, on 24 October 1966 and on 2 December this inaugurated a twice-weekly Taipei–Saigon service. In Indonesia, Nusantara Airlines was formed in 1968 by a group of US and Indonesian businessmen and investors to operate domestic services among the Indonesian islands, as well as limited international services. Plans were made to lease-purchase nine L-1049Hs from Flying Tiger and operations were due to start from Djakarta on 16 September. But Nusantara ran into financial difficulties, its first L-1049H was impounded at Singapore on 21 September and later detained at Hong Kong, and the airline never started operations.

In South America, the Venezuelan operator Linea Expresa Bolivar CA—(LEBCA) acquired two ex-Seaboard L-1049Hs in 1965 for its Caracas–Miami

Bearing the bogus Ghanaian 'registration' 9G-28 for an attempted gun-running flight to the Congo, 1049G N9642Z was formerly Trans-Canada's CF-TEX. It is seen here after being impounded at Luqa, Malta

Also impounded in Malta during mid-1968 because of its part in the Biafran airlift, 1049G 5T-TAF was previously CS-TLC of TAP

scheduled freight services, leasing a third, ex-Slick aircraft the following year and the former TWA L-1049G/H06 N7121C previously used by Flying Tiger. Though made the designated Venezuelan international cargo airline in 1967 LEBCA ceased operations in April 1968. And in Uruguay, CAUSA, which had bought three Model L-749As from KLM in 1962–63 to relace its Short Sandringham flying-boats, had also to suspend operations in 1966 because of financial difficulties. Later, in an attempt to restart operations, CAUSA made plans to purchase two L-1049Hs and leased a third (ex-Resort Airlines) from the Dynalectron Corp, but again the airline ran into financial trouble and its operating permit was cancelled by the Uruguayan Government at the end of 1967.

The Biafra Airlift

When, in May 1967, the breakaway state of Biafra under Col Ojukwu seceded from the rest of Nigeria, the country was plunged into civil war, and it was not long before Biafra was in urgent need of food, arms and medical supplies. Blockaded on land, Biafra turned to the air and by the end of 1967 an airlift was being organised from Lisbon to the main Biafran airstrip at Uli-Ihiala, also known by the code name of 'Annabelle'. Involved in the airlift were four Super Constellations:

an ex-Air France L-1049C, formerly F-BGNE, bearing the bogus Nigerian 'registration' 5N-07G; an ex-Varig L-1049G, which had been sold to the Rhodesian charter operator Air Trans-Africa as VP-WAW; an ex-Iberia and KLM L-1049G, formerly EC-AQN *La Rabida* and now N8025, later given the Mauretanian registration 5T-TAC; and, the fourth, an ex-TAP L-1049G, formerly CS-TLC and now 5T-TAF. The airlift was organised under the auspices of an American, Capt Hank Wharton, and the first four L-1049s were in use for varying periods from June 1967 to mid-February 1968, the airlift costing about £10,000 for each flight and several flights a week usually being made. A fifth L-1049 crashed early in 1968 and, not long afterwards, another was successfully sabotaged while in transit at Bissau, Portuguese Guinea, carrying the wings of a number of Fouga Magister jet trainers destined for the Biafran Air Force.

The Uli airstrip, Biafra's main terminal for most of the war following the capture by Federal forces of Enugu and Port Harcourt airfields, was simply a tarmac roadway in the jungle only 75ft wide with trees and undergrowth extending to within a few feet of the wing-tips of the landing Super Connies. Runway lights were installed on each side of the airstrip, and during the day it was camouflaged with palm branches. With virtually no navaids and in a part of the world notorious for its hostile weather, particularly electrical storms in the heavy rains season, landing a big aeroplane like a Super Connie on such a narrow and primitive airstrip was extremely hazardous at the best of times, and even more so under the constant threat of enemy action. Oddly enough, the major threat came not from the Nigerian Air Force MiG-17 jet fighters and Il-28 jet bombers supplied by Egypt, whose daylight raids could be countered by the airstrip's heavy anti-aircraft defences, but from the six Nigeria Airways DC-3s commandeered by the Nigerian Air Force, four of which were used as night bombers with a crude shute fed by a roller conveyor belt for ejecting bombs out of the cargo doors. Five more DC-3s were later acquired from Sabena for bombing and these aircraft flew almost nightly from Benin City over Uli. Cruising at between 14,000ft and 18,000ft to get above the flak, they would wait for the L-1049s to arrive and warn them on the VHF set that they would be bombed if they continued their approach. The threat was usually enough to persuade the supply aircraft to go back to their bases at Sao Tomé in the Gulf of Guinea or Libreville (Gabon) and pilots who did attempt to land were apt to find a 220lb bomb exploding on the runway ahead of them as soon as they switched on their landing lights. The resulting overshoot involved a further hazard as flak from the airstrip was often directed at the supply aircraft in mistake for the DC-3s. Fortunately for Biafra the DC-3s could not carry bombs of sufficient size to inflict irrepairable runway damage and as their endurance was limited, there came a time when the supply aircraft could slip in unmolested and unload their vital cargoes. The original four L-1049s on the airlift were supplemented and apparently replaced by four more of uncertain origins but bearing the Mauretanian 'registrations' 5T-TAC (not the same as the ex-Iberia and KLM one which had tip tanks and a different livery), 5T-TAG and 5T-TAH. The fourth, N1469C *Angel of Mercy*, was the ex-Slick Airways L-1049H N469C and initially at least had the title 'Transcontinental Airlines SA' on the cabin roof in an attempt at disguise although the airline of that name which had once operated it had been out of business for six years. Another airlift L-1049 was 'registered' 5T-TAK.

A number of international relief agencies also flew a variety of transport aircraft, mostly L-1049s, DC-7s and DC-6s, into Biafra, these being left unmolested by the DC-3 bombers when operating into Uli. The Roman Catholic relief agency, Caritas International, chartered L-1049s from March 1968, which operated from Sao Tomé and were often able to smuggle in two plane-loads a night of medicine and food such as salt, rice, beans and powdered milk. An L-1049 chartered by the Red Cross crashed on landing at night in bad weather on 1 July 1968 with a load of 10½ tons of medical supplies, the three crew and one passenger aboard being killed. And on 3 August 1969 Nordair L-1049H CF-NAJ crashed at Uli while on charter to Canairelief, operated by the Presbyterian Church of Canada and Oxfam of Canada, while CF-NAK was destroyed by strafing at Uli on 17 December of that year. Nordair's other two L-1049Hs were also chartered to Canairelief, while an ex-Transocean and Capitol L-1049H CF-AEN, formerly N1927H, was used by Joint Church Aid. In this curiously ramshackle air war, with DC-3s being used as makeshift bombers and armed light aircraft by Biafra, it was the airlift above all that enabled Biafra to prolong its resistance and hence its agony. Several airlift L-1049s were abandoned by their owners in Africa or at Lisbon after Biafra's surrender in January 1970.

Further Sales

The Rhodesian charter operator, Air Trans-Africa, which had employed an ex-Varig 1049G in the Biafra airlift, acquired a second ex-Thai Airways Super G from TAP at the end of 1968 (this later going to its charter subsidiary Afro-Continental Airways) and transferred its first, VP-WAW, to the Gabon register as TR-LNY and then to Afro-Continental. This had originally been acquired through the South African operator, Protea Airways, and the letters TR-LNY were later allotted to a DC-7C. The US 'non-sked' Central American Airways Flying Service bought an L-1049H from Trans-International to supplement its L-749A, and Flying W Airways of Medford, New Jersey, which controlled Red Dodge Aviation, leased three ex-REAL Aerovias L-1049Hs in 1969 for a time to supplement Red Dodge's fleet of Lockheed Hercules used on North Slope oil exploration support flights in Alaska. Eight ex-Flying Tiger L-1049Hs were also acquired by the North Slope Supply Co of Anchorage, Alaska, in August 1969 (through Murphree Air International) for air transport support of the sizeable oil-drilling operations that had recently begun in Northern Alaska. In Paraguay, a charter operator by the name of Transcontinental SA (not to be confused with the defunct Argentine airline) was operating

Nordair of Montreal bought National's four 1049Hs in 1964 for transatlantic charters and group charters to Jamaica. CF-NAJ seen here crashed at the Uli airstrip in Biafra while on charter to Canairelief

L-1049E/01-55 ZP-TBV for several months in 1968, and the ex-Transocean L-1049H used as CF-AEN in Biafra by Joint Church Aid was later sold to the Greek charter operator, Hellenic Air. A Miami firm, Air Cargo Operations, temporarily acquired an ex-Thai Airways and TAP L-1049G in 1969 and an ex-Qantas L-1049H, both subsequently going to Leasing Consultants of Forest Hills, New York State, for leasing out to other operators. The ex-Qantas one was later left at Faro after participating in the Biafra airlift, together with another L-1049 *Endeavour*, bearing the bogus Nigerian 'registration' 5N-83H (this was formerly CS-TLA of TAP), and a third of unknown identity.

10: The Starliner

By the early 1950s the continual process of stretching the basic Constellation/Super Constellation and DC-6/DC-7 designs through a series of versions of increased fuselage length, payload and range had brought transport aircraft design within reach of a long-desired goal. This was non-stop operation of the North Atlantic route in both directions all the year round, and the ability to make the east-to-west crossing against severe winter headwinds without sacrifice of payload. Already KLM had started operating Super Constellation flights non-stop eastbound from New York to Amsterdam from August 1953, thus offering for the first time a non-stop Atlantic crossing, although not in both directions. In 1954 both Douglas and Lockheed started the design of what were to be their final models in the piston-engined line, both specifically designed for non-stop all-the-year-round operation of the North Atlantic route in both directions, with sufficient fuel capacity to cope with the strongest westerly headwinds without loss of payload. The Douglas solution in the DC-7C was to increase the wing span by 10ft added in the form of a wing-root centre section to accommodate more fuel, to reduce noise by moving the inboard engines 5ft further away from the fuselage, and to increase the fuel capacity to 7,860 US gal from the 6,400 US gal of the DC-7B. The Lockheed approach in the Model L-1449 project (the designation Model 1349 was not used for superstitious reasons) was a more radical one, involving a completely new and redesigned wing of 150ft span with integral fuel tankage for 9,600 US gal, more than twice that of the Model L-049. Wing area was increased by 200sq ft to 1,850sq ft, the aspect ratio was 12·15 instead of the 9·7 of the earlier wing, and thickness/chord ratio was reduced to provide laminar flow as far as possible.

Inevitably, the complete redesign of the wing, coupled with the non-availability of its originally intended turboprop powerplant, meant that the Model L-1649A Starliner (as the production version was finally known) was later than the DC-7C by a whole year in entering North Atlantic service, and sales suffered accordingly.

The Model L-1449, the first new wing version, was intended to be powered by four 6,000ehp (maximum take-off) Pratt & Whitney PT2F-1 turboprops, the civil version of the T-34 tested in the R7V-2 and YC-121F. A number of alternative turboprop powerplants were also considered, including the Rolls-Royce RB.109, later to be named the Tyne, the Pratt & Whitney T-52 (which never went into production), the Allison T-56 and the new Bristol BE.25, later to be named Orion, a very promising new two-shaft engine of very low fuel consumption. The two British engines had not at this stage been test flown, and in any case US airlines would undoubtedly have preferred an American turboprop, while to have chosen the civil version of the Allison T-56, which also powered the Lockheed Electra turboprop on which design work began in 1955, would have resulted in 'unselling' the Electra. So it was that development delays in producing a civil version of the Pratt & Whitney T-34 led to the abandonment of the Model L-1449 project early in 1955. The 1449's cruising speed was estimated at 432mph at 20,000ft at a weight of 150,000lb, and the maximum still air range at 5,300 miles with a 16,460lb payload. Its maximum take-off weight would have been 177,000lb, more than twice that at which the Constellation prototype had made its first flight twenty-one years earlier. Maximum landing weight would have been 123,000lb, and the wing loading 94·3lb/sq ft.

Although it remained a project, the 1449 accounted for a great deal of the design work on new features, particularly the new wing, that later went into the Model L-1649A. The wing, with a major exception, was to be constructed of large integrally-stiffened skin panels up to 37ft long and measuring from $1\frac{3}{4}$in to $\frac{1}{2}$in in thickness, the largest machined panels so far built for a transport aircraft. A single integrally-stiffened sheet skin runs from the root to the tip between the spars on both upper and lower surfaces, and between the spars the whole wing comprises a vast torsion box

The new 150ft-span wing of the Model 1649A was not only thinner and of higher aspect ratio but set further back on the fuselage

used for fuel tankage as far as the outer engine nacelles. There full-depth tank-end wing ribs form the ends of the four-tank fuel system, very closely spaced ribs being a characteristic of the wing structure. Each half-wing was continuous from the aircraft's centre-line to the tip, and on the Model 1649A the single skin panel between the spars was replaced by five 24in panels top and bottom at the wing root, adjacent sections being joined by double rows of rivets. The wing trailing edges and flaps were revised, the tailplane chord slightly increased to reduce the thickness/chord ratio to a point comparable with that of the wing, and the tailplane span was increased. The wing leading edge sub-structure was arranged to hinge upwards as far as the outer engines to provide access to various interior services, and on the 1449 de-icing would have been by hot air bled from the turboprop compressors. The control surfaces were hydraulically boosted by a new model of Eclipse-Pioneer hydraulic booster similar to the units used on the C-130 Hercules.

With the new wing went undercarriage main legs of new design and considerably more massive construction to cater for the higher gross weights and to allow

its use as a speed brake at indicated airspeeds of up to 269mph; the nose leg was also strengthened. The Model 1449 would have featured the standard Super Constellation fuselage lengthened by 4ft 7in to give a length (with weather radar fitted) of 120ft 9in, and typical cabin interiors were a 60-seat first-class layout with a four-seat lounge (or 70 first-class on the US domestic routes) or an 89-seater all-tourist interior, the capacity payload being 20,000lb.

About a month after design of the Model L-1449 had begun, development started of the Model L-1549, very similar to it and likewise featuring the new wing and Pratt & Whitney PT2F-1 turboprops. The fuselage, however, was to be 10ft 9in longer than that of the Super Constellation without weather radar, giving an overall length of 124ft 4in. The proposed maximum gross weight now went up to 187,500lb, the Model 1549 being the heaviest Constellation variant ever to be projected, and the wing loading would have been just over 100lb/sq ft. Accommodation for 60–75 first-class passengers or up to ninety tourists would have been provided, although more could have been carried in a high-density layout making use of all the available extra fuselage length. A payload of about 18,000lb could have been carried over 4,000 miles at 410mph at 30,000ft, but apparently this was not considered a sufficient advance over the existing Super

Constellation variants to have made the L-1549 a commercial proposition and this, together with delay in development of the T-34/PT2F-1 turboprop, led to its being abandoned along with the Model 1449 early in 1955.

ASA International Airlines, or Aerovias Sud Americana Inc, which operated scheduled freight services from Miami to Central and South America, and which had suspended operations in July 1965 when a bankruptcy petition was filed, was planning to resume operations in 1966 with three L-1649As converted into freighters and re-engined with turboprops, as well as three Boeing 727QC jets. But in the end nothing came of these plans as ASA International was unable to restart operations (it had previously operated three ex-TWA Model L-049s, amongst other types), in spite of Airlift International acquiring a 42 per cent financial stake in it.

Following the demise of the Models 1449 and 1549, work began in earnest in May 1955 on the Model L-1649, later designated L-1649A, and known at first as the Super Constellation, then renamed Super Star Constellation and later, from March 1957, the Starliner. The earlier name had been dropped because it was thought to be too long, though TWA called its 1649As Jetstream Starliners to capitalise on the publicity appeal of the word 'jet', if only obliquely. The L-1649A was claimed by Lockheed to have the greatest range of any airliner, and to be able to to fly from Paris to New

Comparison of wing plan forms and nacelle centrelines of Model 1049G and 1649A

York in nearly three hours less time than the DC-7C when carrying the same payload. It was also claimed to be 70mph faster than any other piston-engined airliner at ranges of over 4,200 miles, and capable of bringing every European capital within non-stop reach of New York. In place of the PT2F-1 turbo-props intended for the 1449 and 1549, the 1649A reverted to Turbo-Compounds, being powered by four 3,400bhp (maximum take-off) R-3350-988TC18 EA-2 engines mounted 5ft 2·6in further outboard from the cabin than previous models. Cabin noise was further reduced by the choice of an airscrew reduction gear ratio of 0·355 instead of 0·4375 and larger diameter, low tip-speed Hamilton Standard airscrews (16ft 10in instead of 15ft 2in).

Two types of Hamilton Standard airscrew were offered for the 1649A, the Model 43H60/HA17A3-4 with hollow dural blades and the Model 43H60/6993-B4 with solid dural blades, the former giving a weight saving of 680lb per aircraft but costing nearly twice as much as the other version. Initially, TWA chose the hollow-blade model but soon replaced them by the solid-blade version after running into problems with the nylon foam core material of the hollow blades. Air France chose Curtiss Electric airscrews for its L-1949A fleet. Cabin soundproofing was further improved by the addition of 900lb of insulating material and this, together with the synchrophasing of the airscrews, helped to achieve a cabin that was even quieter than that of the Model 1049G.

With its design emphasis on range rather than payload, the 1649A could carry 58-64 passengers in a four-abreast first-class layout or thirty-two in a de luxe interior or up to ninety-nine coach-class, a typical mixed interior seating twenty-six first-class plus forty-five tourist passengers. A payload of 17,000lb could be carried over a still-air range of 5,300 miles at a cruising speed of about 350mph. Unlike the Models 1449 and 1549, the 1649A featured no fuselage stretch, the length with weather radar installed being 116ft 2in, or the same as the Super Constellation's. The total fuel capacity was 9,600 US gal and the fuel lines were placed inside the tanks. There were two fully independent hydraulic systems, each operating at 3,000lb/sq in, and for the control surfaces Eclipse-Pioneer hydraulic control boosters similar to those on the C-130 Hercules. Stronger main under-carriage legs as first schemed for the Model 1449 were

incorporated and Goodyear Tri-Metallic disc brakes could be fitted. The 1649A's maximum gross weight of 156,000lb was considerably less than that of the 1449 or 1549 projects and the maximum landing weight was 123,000lb, the payload (space-limited) being 17,130lb on US domestic routes or 16,428lb on international routes. The zero fuel weight was 116,000lb and maximum gross weight was later increased to 160,000lb. The flight deck was laid out for two pilots, a radio officer to port facing aft and a flight engineer to starboard, with a navigator's position to port further aft, separated from the rest of the crew by a bulkhead. Opposite the navigator was a crew rest area with a settee or two rest bunks, and the basic crew arrangement was not very different from that of the Model L-049.

The 1649A prototype, appropriately registered N1649, was rolled out on 19 September, 1956 and made its first flight on 11 October from Burbank, California. The flight was of fifty minutes' duration and the aircraft was piloted by Roy Wimmer with Herman R. Salmon as co-pilot. The second aircraft (the first for TWA) was used in the 86-hour flight-test programme before test flying for CAA certification got under way, and the cabins of both aircraft were full of test instrumentation. A third aircraft was used as a static test airframe. The prototype made 130 flights totalling 165 hours over a period of fifty-one days to qualify for its CAA certificate and early flights revealed a hydraulic 'plumbing' problem, causing sub-standard brake operation, which was put right by the redesign of a pump.

The first deliveries to TWA, which had ordered twenty-five, were made in April 1957 and the airline had ten by 14 June. The next major customer, Air France, whose original order for twelve had been reduced to ten, took delivery of its first 1649A on 9 July 1957, this aircraft flying non-stop from Los Angeles to Paris in the record-breaking time of 17hr 11min for the 5,800 miles journey. Air France's 1649As were fitted with RCA AVQ-10 weather radar and special tourist seats designed by the airline itself. A three-class interior with thirty-four tourist seats, twelve first-class Sky-lounge sleeper seats and eight Pullman-style sleeping-berths was featured, which could be converted to forty-four Sky-lounge seats and six berths for the new trans-Polar route from Paris to Tokyo via Anchorage (Alaska) which the airline

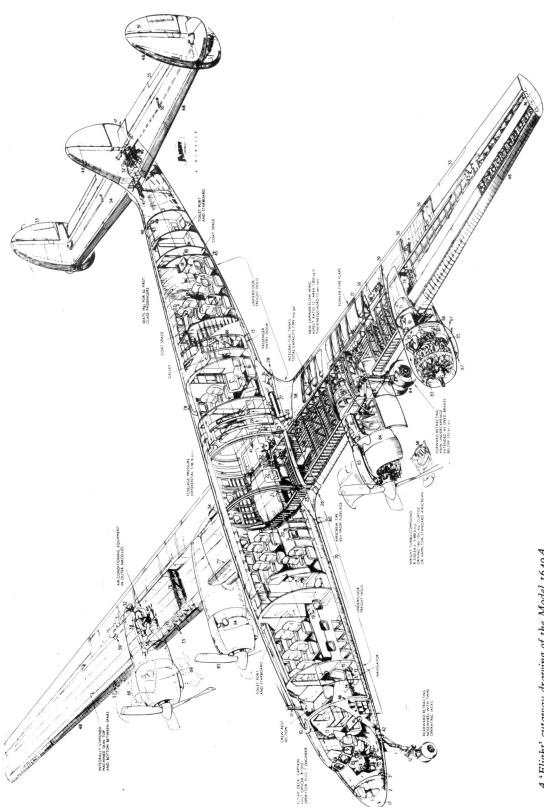

A 'Flight' cutaway drawing of the Model 1649A
showing the main structural features and arrangement
of accommodation

III

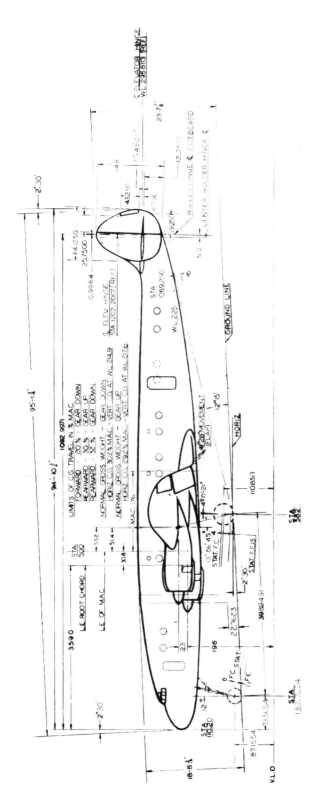

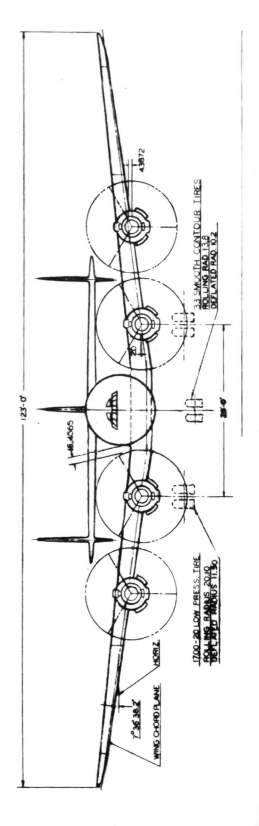

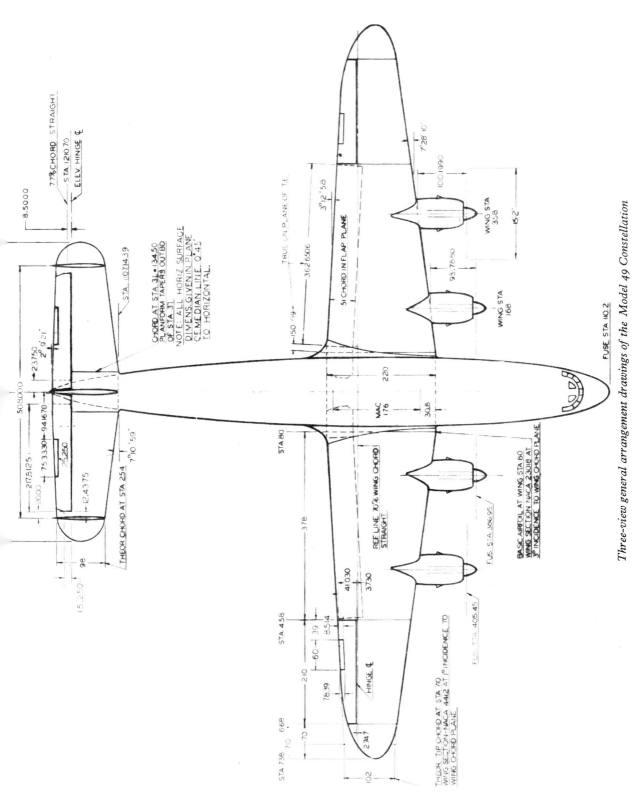

Three-view general arrangement drawings of the Model 49 Constellation

Seen in this night shot at Orly airport are Air France's 1649A F-BHBO Champlain *and 1049G F-BHML*

inaugurated on 10 April 1958. Air France called its 1649As Super Starliners.

In March 1956 two other European carriers, Deutsche Lufthansa and Linee Aeree Italiane (LAI) of Italy each ordered four Model L-1649As; LAI's were to have been named *Roman, Ambrosian, Vesuvian* and *Sicilian* and to have operated what would have been the world's longest non-stop airline service from Rome to New York, a distance of 4,280 miles, taking 12hr eastbound and 15hr 30min for the westbound crossing. LAI was due to receive its first 1649A in October 1957 and had specified Hamilton Standard airscrews with solid dural blades. At this time there were still two separate Italian airlines for the major international routes, LAI, in which TWA had a 40 per cent interest

(which may have influenced its choice of the 1649A) and which operated a European network and to the Middle East and the important Rome–New York route, and Alitalia, in which BEA had a 30 per cent interest, operating European routes and to South America, East Africa and South Africa. But it was becoming increasingly clear that Italy's air transport interests were not best served by two separate airlines and with the prospect of having to finance the purchase of jets in a few years time a merger became logical. This came about when LAI was formally liquidated in August 1957 and the new airline, Alitalia-LAI, was incorporated on 1 September and took over LAI's operations on 6 October. Alitalia had ordered DC-7Cs before the merger and so the LAI 1649As were added to TWA's fleet. TWA surrendered its financial interest in the airline, and BEA eventually sold its interest in Alitalia in April 1961.

Lufthansa's first 1649A landed at Hamburg on 3 October 1957 after flying 7,000 miles non-stop from Burbank in 17hr 19min—a dramatic illustration of the extra range conferred by the new wing. Lufthansa put its 1649As, which it called Super Star Constellations, on to the USA and Canada routes, and also on services to South America and the Near and Middle East. The transatlantic services at first featured a three-class de luxe, first and tourist interior, followed later by a de luxe 32-seat interior with which Lufthansa introduced their twice-weekly 'The Senator' prestige service to the USA.

After they were displaced as first-line equipment by the 707s introduced in 1960, two of the Lufthansa 1649As, D-ALAN and D-ALUB, were converted into freighters from April 1960 by Lockheed Aircraft Services with the upward-opening freight doors fore and aft of the Model L-1049H and the latter's heavy duty floor and cargo tie-down points. These were then sold, in 1962, to the US supplemental World Airways. The other two 1649As were transferred to Lufthansa's wholly-owned charter subsidiary, Condor Flugdienst, which flew group charter and inclusive tour flights to points in Europe, North Africa and the Mediterranean. In June 1956 Varig of Brazil ordered two Model L-1649As for the Buenos Aires–New York route for delivery beginning in December 1957, but this order was later changed to a repeat one for three more L-1049Gs as Varig decided to standardise on this

version. The 1649As were to have seated 33–45 first-class passengers in a special de luxe 'siesta' interior with eight berths in the rear compartment.

Meanwhile TWA had introduced Model 1649A services, known as 'The Jetstream', across the Atlantic on 1 July 1957 and by the end of the month these were linking New York to London and also Frankfurt, Paris and Rome. A 74-passenger all-tourist interior was featured for the Atlantic services and a two-class interior accommodating thirty first-class and thirty-four tourist passengers for the US transcontinental routes, with a central first-class sleeping compartment with four upper and four lower berths. The 1649As operated the 'Non-Stop Ambassador' from New York to Los Angeles and San Francisco non-stop, as well as a Boston–Los Angeles flight from mid-August, and a Washington–San Francisco service. And on 2 October 1957 TWA inaugurated an over-the-Pole 1649A service between Los Angeles and London via San Francisco, three weeks after Pan American had started the same route with DC-7s but three years before BOAC's 707s began flying over the Pole between London and Los Angeles. In March 1958 a TWA 1649A achieved the record time of 19hr 5min on a non-stop London–San Francisco flight with eighteen

Lufthansa 1649A D-ALOL was transferred to Condor Flugdienst and later went to World Airways and Trek Airways

passengers and ten crew aboard, beating the previous best 1649A time of 23hr 20min set up the previous October. The cabin arrangement for the US transcontinental flights was later changed to forty-four first-class and twenty coach-class seats and from 14 October 1957 TWA introduced a new de luxe facility on these flights by converting the first-class section to take thirty-two sleeper seats, a 'Starlight Lounge' being a feature of the US domestic flights. The 1649A and 1049G transcontinental coach services were also known as 'Golden Banner' services, the name 'Sky Chief' was applied to first-class services on other Constellations, and 'Sky Club' was the name applied to the Model L-049 Constellation coach-class services, most of these aircraft now being operated with 81-passenger air coach interiors. In 1959, TWA's entire 1649A fleet was operated in an economy/coach-class configuration.

In 1960 six of the Jetstream Starliners were converted into freighters by Lockheed Aircraft Services, with a forward cargo door 4ft 8½in wide × 6ft high and a rear door 8ft 10½in wide × 6ft high, both opening upwards, and a strengthened freight floor, the transatlantic cargo payload now being 37,250lb. These started to replace the L-1049Hs on TWA's transcontinental and transatlantic freight services from August 1960, and in 1961 six more 1649As were converted to freighters. With the introduction of Boeing 707s in 1959, TWA's 1649As were gradually displaced as first-line equipment, the last international service with the type, from Cairo to New York, being flown on 28 October 1961. The 1649A was withdrawn from the US domestic routes the following year, although the converted freighters continued transatlantic cargo flights until 1963 and US domestic services for four years after that. TWA's last flight with any of the Constellation series was made by L-1649A freighter N7315C on 11 May 1967 and its last passenger flight with the type (and last piston-engined flight with any type) had been flown between New York and Kansas City on 6 April 1967 by Model L-749A N6024C *Star of Nebraska*. The year 1959 had seen the peak of TWA's Constellation operations, with a total fleet of no less than 147 in service, made up of thirty-two L-049s, twelve L-749s, twenty-seven L-749As, nine L-1049As, twenty-eight L-1049Gs, nine L-1049Hs and twenty-nine L-1649As. An estimated 50 million passengers were flown in TWA Constellations between

1946 and 1967. In the end only forty-three Model L-1649As were built plus the prototype, and in spite of its ability to operate very long stages such as London–San Francisco non-stop this new wing variant was heavily outsold by the DC-7C (of which 121 were built).

Second-Hand Sales

As the 1649A was essentially a stop-gap between the Super Constellation and the big jets, it was not long before the first examples began to come on to the used airliner market. TWA sold four to a new Argentine carrier, Trans Atlantica Argentina, in 1960–61 on a lease-purchase basis, the first being sold on 12 September 1960, and with these a twice-weekly service between Buenos Aires and Geneva via Rio de Janeiro, Recife and Lisbon was started, Dakar later being substituted for Recife as a stop. But as more of the established airlines, such as Aerolineas Argentinas, introduced jets between South America and Europe, it became impossible to operate profitably over this route with piston-engined types, and Trans Atlantica Argentina had to suspend operations on 5 November 1961.

Another TWA 1649A was acquired from a Miami aircraft dealer in the spring of 1964 for long-haul freight charters by the Argentine charter operator, Lineas Aereas Patagonica Argentinas SRL (LAPA), which had also acquired an ex-TWA L-1049A and an ex-Seaboard L-1049D. But LAPA had got into economic difficulties and suspended all its flights in September 1965, finally ceasing operations when its L-1049A crashed off Lima on a smuggling flight on 6 March 1966. Another ex-TWA 1649A was leased by the Argentine scheduled freight carrier, Aerovias Halcon SRL, for a time from May 1968; this airline operated freight services within Argentina, to seven other South American countries and to Miami. Yet another ex-TWA 1649A was acquired in 1966 on lease from Passaat of Miami for one flight by Aerovias Condor de Colombia Ltda—(Aerocondor), which operates scheduled domestic services and to Aruba, Curacao and Miami, but this crashed on 18 December 1966 on the approach to Bogota's El Dorado airport.

Air France leased a 1649A to Air Afrique in October 1961 and two more from 18 April 1962, the latter being re-registered in the Ivory Coast as TU-TBB and TU-TBA and returned to Air France on (respectively)

28 May and 7 June 1963. Air Afrique was the multi-national airline of eleven newly-independent former French African states to which both Air France and the French independent UAT provided technical assistance and aircraft, including 707 and DC-8 jets, as well as DC-6Bs and DC-4s. The South African carrier Trek Airways, which specialised in the operation of low-fare, low-frequency services from South Africa to Europe, acquired two ex-Lufthansa 1649As from World Airways Inc in February and March 1964, and operated them on scheduled flights from Johannesburg to Luxembourg, having been made the designated South African carrier on this route, for which Luxembourg was now the main European terminal.

Trek's flights were routed through Windhoek, Luanda (Angola) and the Cape Verde Islands to circumvent the anti-apartheid ban on South African aircraft overflying their territories imposed by the black African states in the summer of 1963, and the 1649A's extra range enabled this new routeing to be flown with a full payload; the Windhoek stop was later dropped. A co-operative agreement was signed with the Luxembourg airline, Luxair, for joint operation of the 1649As from April 1964, Luxair operating a connecting Luxembourg–London flight with the 1649As, all three of which (the third was acquired from Air France in April 1966) were re-registered in Luxembourg. On 7 May 1965, Trek began a once-fortnightly 1649A service on behalf of South African Airways from Johannesburg to Perth via Mauritius and the Cocos Islands, this alternating with SAA's

DC-7B service over the same route to provide a weekly South African frequency to match the weekly Qantas Electra service to Johannesburg; the Trek 1649A flights over the Indian Ocean route continued until September 1965. The 1649As, which were operated as 98-seaters, were replaced on flights to Luxembourg by a leased Britannia from June 1968, but a 1649A operated the onward flight to London until 30 September of that year; later a 707 replaced the Britannia and the 1649As were used for charter flights from South Africa.

TWA leased two 1649A freighters to Alaska Airlines during 1962–63 for the latter's MATS contract charter work, Alaska finally buying them both on 31 December 1963 and a third, for spares, in March 1965 to supplement its L-1049Hs. After 1965 the 1649As were also used for certain scheduled services such as those between Anchorage and Fairbanks, and both the Alaska aircraft, plus a third ex-TWA 1649A freighter, were disposed of in 1969 to the Prudhoe Bay Oil Distributing Co of Anchorage, one of the companies associated with the big oil-drilling operations in northern Alaska. Prudhoe Bay later turned over one of these 1649As to Red Dodge Aviation, a subsidiary of Flying W Airways.

The travel clubs that sprang up in the States in the mid-1960s to provide cheap air transport for their

The Air Venturers travel club operated 1649A N179AV, previously N45512 of World and D-ALAN of Lufthansa. It was leased for a few months from October 1966 to Trans-Mediterranean Airways of Beirut for freighting

members in the piston-engined airliners now made obsolete by jets, used the 1649A as well as the earlier model Constellations. World Samplers acquired one of TWA's through a dealer in November 1965, and had previously leased the one that later crashed with Aerocondor of Colombia besides using a Model 049, the other one being registered to the Association of Flying Travel Clubs in 1967. Another travel club, Flying Ambassadors, were operating an ex-TWA 1649A in 1966, and an unexpected buyer of one of TWA's Jetstream Starliners was the Moral Rearmament organisation, which bought N7314C on 10 December 1965. It did not keep it for long, for in 1966 it was in use by the International Travel Club, which gave it the tongue-twisting name of *Supercalifragilistic-expealidocious*. It later went to another travel club known as Holiday Wings, and was painted with the legend 'West Texas Flying Clubhouse'. One of the ex-Lufthansa 1649A freighters used by World Airways went to a travel club called Air Venturers on 3 March 1966 but in October of that year it was leased to the Lebanese all-freight carrier, Trans Mediterranean Airways SAL, to supplement DC-6s and DC-4s on the airline's cargo services between Beirut and London. In February 1967 the lease ended and it returned to the States to a company called Tex Hou and then to the CHS Leasing Corporation.

World Airways acquired all four of the ex-Lufthansa 1649As on lease, two in July and two in October 1962, to supplement its L-1049Hs. Two of these went to

World Airways 1649A N45520 seen here was previously D-ALOL illustrated on page 115; it later went to Trek as ZS-DVJ

Trek early in 1964, when the leases on the others expired, one later went to Air Venturers and the fourth went back to Lufthansa to be finally retired by them in November 1965, eventually ending its days converted into a restaurant at Hartenholm, near Hamburg. Two of the ex-TWA 1649As went to a company called Willair International but one was scrapped after an undercarriage collapse at Stockton, California in September 1968, and one of the Luxair/Trek aircraft, LX-LGY (formerly F-BHBR) became N4796 in July 1969 and was given the Icelandic registration TF-ERA for a single flight to Tel Aviv in the colours of a charter operator called Nittler Air Transport International, although the registered owner was Bjorn Sverrisson. It later left Luxembourg and was registered in Panama as HP-501 in October 1969. Another operator was Air Korea, which acquired 1649A freighter HL-4003 in March 1967 and used it on charter flights in the Far East until operations ceased in August 1968.

One of the ex-TWA 1649As later used by Trans Atlantica Argentina, N7307C (formerly LV-GLI), was returned to TWA early in 1964 and sold by them to the FAA for the low price of $38,000 for a simulated air crash at Deer Valley Airport, Phoenix, Arizona, which was staged on 3 September 1964; a DC-7 was also used in a similar crash test. The purpose of these tests was to provide comprehensive data to help reduce the hazards of landing and take-off accidents and to study under full-scale, simulated conditions factors affecting passenger survival and evacuation, impact and fire damage and spread. The tests were made by the Flight Safety Foundation under an FAA contract, and both the DC-7 and 1649A were fully instrumented to

record fuel tank pressures, wing and fuselage accelerations and crash loads and stresses. Detailed experiments were designed to obtain data on passenger and crew seat strength and restraint systems, cargo restraint systems and methods of fuel containment. High-speed ciné cameras in the cabin were used to photograph the effect of the impact on seats and twenty-one dummy passengers, while external cameras covered the overall impact sequence and the rupturing of the fuel tanks. A number of extra window–like squares were painted on the 1649A's fuselage for observation purposes, these stretching right back to the tailplane leading edge and forward over the nosewheel bay, there being a second line of such squares underneath the first on the forward fuselage.

To simulate the crash the 1649A and DC-7 were started, the engines being warmed up and the instrumentation switched on. Engine power was then increased by remote control to accelerate the aircraft up to about 140mph before it struck a series of prepared barriers, the 1649A being guided to the crash site by means of a guide rail and an attachment to the nosewheel to ensure that it followed the correct path without any pilots on board; it was, however, just airborne for half a second before impact. The port wing struck an inclined mound of earth intended to provide the progressive destruction of the wing as would occur in a touchdown with one wing too low, the

Bearing the Panamanian registration HP-501, this 1649A was previously F-BHBR of Air France and LX-LGY of Luxair

starboard wing then colliding with two telephone wire poles representing trees. The fuselage crashed into a shallow hill sloping at about 10 degrees, this slope extending for a distance of 150ft, levelling out for another 150ft and then rising again at an angle of 20 degrees. The aircraft came to rest some 300ft beyond the wing crash barriers, the fuselage breaking some way aft of the cockpit and again about two-thirds of the way along its length. Later the partly wrecked fuselage, still where it came to rest on final impact, was used for a series of tests on emergency passenger evacuation, beginning on 8 April 1965 with volunteers from the Deer Valley area acting as 'passengers' and selected to reflect the composition of a typical airline flight—57 per cent male, 30 per cent female, 5 per cent of both sexes aged sixty or more and 8 per cent children under twelve. To achieve the greatest possible realism, passenger injuries were faked, the cabin aisles were deliberately cluttered and smoke bombs and crash sound effects were added, the breaks in the fuselage from the crash being covered over. Again, remotely-controlled ciné cameras were used both outside and inside the aircraft to record passenger reaction, and various parts of the evacuation process were precisely timed. These tests were also conducted by the Flight

Model 1649A N7307C after the FAA's simulated air crash test at Deer Valley Airport, showing the emergency exits open over the wing and just aft of the rear fuselage break. No. 3 engine is on the ground behind the shattered starboard wing

Safety Foundation under FAA contract, and were used to plan advanced studies of evacuation procedures.

A Truly Classic Airliner

Production of the 1649A had proceeded in parallel with that of the Model L-1049H and, with the cancellation of the US Navy W2V-1 radar picket version of the 1649A in 1957, did not extend beyond the forty-three airline aircraft built. The last Connie to be built was completed in late 1958 and the last delivery to an airline was that of Model L-1049H N6935C to Slick Airways on 30 September 1959. A grand total of 856 Connies were built, of which 623 were Super Constellations and 1649As (232 of these were RC-121/EC-121 early warning versions) and design and development of the basic series is estimated by Lockheed to have taken 20,258,118 man-hours to the end of 1955. This represents a sum of over $100 million spent on the engineering aspects alone of the Constellation series up to the end of 1955 at an average cost per man-hour of $5·00, not including various supplementary testing and material changes. In 1955 a total of 16,800 Lockheed employees owed their jobs to the Constellation programme, apart from many others at Lockheed Aircraft Services engaged in modification and maintenance work. At this time the company expected to be building improved models of the type into the mid-1960s but this was not to be, partly because of the lack of a suitable American turboprop for the thin wing 1649A and also because attention was now focused on the new Electra turboprop for which American Airlines had placed the first order (for thirty-five) in June 1955.

The price of a Constellation had steadily increased as the type was developed, the L-049 costing about $700,000 (£175,000) and later $800,000 (£200,000), the L-749 and 749A costing about $1 million (£250,000) in 1950, and the L-1049G from $1,920,000 to $2,070,000 (£680,000 to £740,000). The 1649A was the most expensive, originally costing about $2,500,000 (£900,000) but later selling at $2,350,000 (£840,000). In 1962, probably the most active year for the used Constellation market, the current asking price of an L-049 had fallen to about £40,000, an L-749A £60,000, an L-1049C to about £100,000 and an L-1049G £150,000. The Constellation's low price led it into a number of smuggling ventures and into the hands of not a few under-capitalised and short-lived operators on both sides of the Atlantic, but whether flying arms into the Yemen or Biafra, or illicit cargoes into Latin American republics, or flying US transcontinental, North Atlantic or the Qantas round-the-world services with fare-paying passengers, the Lockheed Constellation never failed to demonstrate its qualities as one of the truly classic airliners.

Appendices

APPENDIX 1   CONSTELLATION SPECIFICATIONS: 1

Dimensions (Models 049 to 749A): Span, 123ft 0in; length, 95ft $1\frac{3}{16}$in; height, 23ft 0in; wing area, 1,650sq ft; aspect ratio, 9·7; dihedral, 7° 36′; undercarriage track, 28ft 0in; wheelbase, 33ft 1in.

Cabin dimensions (Models 049 to 749A): Cabin volume, 3,000cu ft; underfloor freight hold volume, 434cu ft; cabin length, 64ft 9in; max internal diameter, 132in; max height, 6ft 6in; max usable floor area, 561sq ft.

	Model 049	049E	649	749	749A
Weights					
Empty	51,400lb		58,073lb	58,643lb	60,141lb
Equipped weight			61,000lb	61,500lb	
Max payload	13,800lb	18,423lb	11,636lb		20,276lb
Max landing weight	77,280lb	84,500lb	84,500lb	87,500lb	89,500lb
Max gross weight	90,000lb	98,000lb	94,000lb	102,000lb	107,000lb
Wing loading	54·5lb/sq ft	59·4lb/sq ft	56·9lb/sq ft	61·8lb/sq ft	64·8lb/sq ft
Power loading	10·2lb/bhp	9·8lb/bhp	9·4lb/bhp	10·2lb/bhp	10·7lb/bhp

	Model 049	649	749	749A
Performance				
Max speed	340mph	352mph	352mph	
Cruising speed	280–320mph	321mph at 23,000ft	309mph at 23,000ft	304mph at 20,000ft
Take-off run to clear 50ft	2,800ft	3,090ft	5,049ft	
Landing run from 50ft	2,300ft	2,499ft	2,499ft	4,670ft
Service ceiling	24,600ft	25,700ft	24,100ft	
Initial rate of climb	1,500ft/min	1,480ft/min	1,280ft/min	
Landing speed	93mph	88mph	88mph	
Range	2,850 miles with 13,800lb payload	3,200 miles (still air) at 323mph at 20,000ft with 3,680lb payload	3,900 miles (still air) at 320mph at 20,000ft with 4,185lb payload	3,800 miles with max payload or 4,840 miles with max fuel and 8,026lb payload

CONSTELLATION SPECIFICATIONS: 2

Dimensions (Models 1049A to 1049H): Span, 123ft 0in; length, 113ft 4in (without weather radar), 116ft 2in (with weather radar); height, 24ft 9in; wing area, 1,650sq ft; aspect ratio, 9·7; dihedral, 7° 36′; undercarriage track, 28ft 0in; wheelbase, 43ft 11in.

Dimensions (Model 1649A): As above except for span, 150ft 0in; height, 23ft 5in; wing area, 1,850sq ft; aspect ratio, 12·15; dihedral, 7° 36′; undercarriage track, 38ft 5in; wheelbase, 49ft 2in.

Cabin dimensions (Models 1049A to 1649A): Cabin volume, 4,800cu ft (1049 series), 4,875cu ft (1649A); under-floor freight hold volume, 728cu ft (1049 series) 593cu ft (1649A); cabin length, 83ft 2in (1049 series), 85ft 9in (1649A); max internal diameter, 132in; max height, 6ft 6in; max usable floor area, 744sq ft.

	Model 1049A	1049E	1049G	1049H	1649A
Weights					
Empty		70,167lb			85,553lb
Equipped weight	69,000lb (approx.)	76,423lb	79,237lb		91,806lb
Max payload	22,500lb (approx.)		24,293lb	40,203lb (5% overload)	17,130lb
Zero fuel weight		103,500lb	108,000lb		116.000lb
Max landing weight	98,500lb	110,000lb	113,000lb	113,000lb	123,000lb
Max gross weight	120,000lb	133,000lb	137,500lb	137,500lb	156,000lb
Wing loading	72·5lb/sq ft	80·6lb/sq ft	83·4lb/sq ft	84·3lb/sq ft	84·3lb/sq ft
Power loading	11·1lb/bhp	10·2lb/bhp	10·58lb/bhp	10·58lb/bhp	11·5lb/bhp

Performance	Model 1049A	1049E	1049G	1649A
Max speed	over 330mph	376mph at 20,000ft at 110,000lb weight	370mph at 20,000ft	377mph at 18,600ft
Cruising speed	327mph at 65% power	331mph at 23,000ft at 75% power	310mph at 20,000ft at 131,000lb weight	323mph at 20,000ft at 123,000lb weight
Balanced field length (ISA at sea level)		6,100ft	5,800ft	6,250ft
Landing run from 50ft	2,592ft	3,550ft	5,270ft	6,000ft
Service ceiling	over 22,000ft	27,200ft		23,700ft
Initial rate of climb		1,140ft/min		1,080ft/min
Landing speed	95mph	99·5mph		
Range	5,150 miles (max.)	4,820 miles at 10,000ft with no reserves	4,160 miles with max payload or 4,810 miles with max fuel and 18,315lb payload	5,400 miles with max payload or 6,280 miles with max fuel and 10,777lb payload

CONSTELLATION VARIANTS

Model	
L–49	Original Constellation project of April 1939.
L–49–10	Laid down for TWA but completed as C–69–1–LO and C–69–5–LO transports for USAAF; 20 built plus two C–69–10–LOs sold to TWA before delivery to the USAAF.
L–49–43–11	C–69A project to carry 100 troops.
149	Transoceanic variant ordered by Pan Am in 1940. Model number later used for 049 fitted with 749 outer wings.
51 or 249	XB–30 projected heavy bomber derivative; Model 151 was a similar version. Designation L–249 also used for El Al's refurbished 049s.
349	C–69B project for 94 troops or cargo; max gross weight 94,000lb.
449	Proposed redesign of C–69 for airline use of July 1943.
549	C–69C–1–LO transport seating 43 passengers. One delivered; 49 cancelled.
49	C–69D 63-seater. Three ordered and cancelled.
49	XC–69E. Prototype Constellation re-engined with P & W R–2800–34 Double Wasps.
049	War-surplus C–69s converted for the airlines. Max gross weight 86,250lb; landing weight 75,000lb.
049A	049 with strengthened front spar and main undercarriage side struts to allow max gross weight of 90,000lb and landing weight of 77,280lb.
049B	049A with fuselage external stiffeners and stronger main undercarriage for max gross weight of 93,000lb and landing weight of 77,800lb.
049C	049B with undercarriage drag strut damper and modified elevator boost control. Max gross weight of 93,000lb and landing weight of 83,000lb.
049D	First true commercial version. Modified forward fuselage and nosewheel leg, reinforced inner wing for max gross weight of 96,000lb and landing weight of 83,000lb.

Model	
049E	Max gross weight raised to 98,000lb and landing weight to 84,500lb by further 'beefing up'.
149	049 fitted with 749's outer wings to bring fuel capacity to 5,820 US gal. Max gross weight 100,000lb; landing weight 83,000lb.
649	More powerful 'BD–1 engines, improved passenger accommodation. Fuel capacity 4,690 US gal. Max gross weight 94,500lb and landing weight 84,500lb. 14 built for Eastern.
649A	649 with inner wing and main landing gear strengthened for max gross weight of 98,000lb and landing weight of 89,500lb. Superseded by 749.
749	649 with additional fuel tank in each outer wing to bring fuel capacity to 5,820 US gal. Max gross weight 102,000lb (later 105,000lb) and landing weight 87,500lb.
749	C–121A–1–LO personnel transports (8 built), one VC–121A–1–LO and one VC–121B–1–LO VVIP transport. Could also carry stretcher cases or freight. C–121As later modified to VC–121B standard.
749A	Main landing gear and centre section strengthened for max gross weight of 107,000lb and landing weight of 89,500lb.
749A	PO–1W (later WV–1) with dorsal and ventral radomes for early warning role. Two built; later used by FAA for navaid calibration with radomes removed.
749B	Projected version of 749A with the more powerful CA–1 engines of the Model 1049A.
849	Proposed version of 749 with R–3350 Turbo-Compounds and all-up weight of 110,000lb.
749	Air Freighter all-cargo version of 749 projected with P & W R–2800 Double Wasps.

SUPER CONSTELLATION VARIANTS

Model	
949	Military or civil version projected of the 749 with 12ft longer fuselage and 2,250bhp Turbo-Compounds. Max gross weight 123,000lb. Speedfreighter was an all-cargo version.
1049A	Super Constellation with 18ft 4¾in longer fuselage and 2,700bhp 'CB–1 engines. Fuel capacity 6,550 US gal. Max gross weight 120,000lb and landing weight 98,500lb. 24 built.
1049A	WV–2 (ex-PO–2W) and later EC–121K early warning version with dorsal and ventral radomes. Tip tanks and R–3350–34 Turbo-Compounds; fuel capacity 7,750 US gal. Max gross weight 145,000lb.
1049A	WV–3, later WC–121N 'hurricane hunter' version of WV–2. Eight built.
1049A	WV–2E, later EC–121L. Fitted with APS–70 radar in a 40ft dish radome; ventral radome deleted. One built.
1049A	WV–2Q, later EC–121M. Electronic countermeasures version of WV–2.

Model	
1049A–55	RC–121D. As RC–121C but with 1,000 US gal fuel tank in fuselage plus tip tanks to give 8,750 US gal fuel capacity. Interior changes. Max gross weight 143,600lb. 72 built.
1049B–55	R7V–1 (ex-R7O–1) transport for US Navy (later C–121J) with wing structure redesigned for max gross weight of 130,000lb (later 133,000lb). Cargo doors and heavy duty freight floor. R–3350–34W Turbo-Compounds. 50 ordered.
1049B–55	33 R7V–1s transferred to USAF as C–121Gs.
1049B	Commercial freighter version of R7V–1 with max gross weight of 130,000lb. Superseded by 1049D.
1049B–84	RC–121C, the USAF version of the WV–2. R–3350–93 Turbo-Compounds. Max gross weight 127,264lb. Ten built.
1049C	First civil Turbo-Compound version with 'DA–1 engines and Dreyfuss-styled interiors. Fuel capacity 6,550 US gal. Max gross weight 133,000lb. Max landing weight 110,000lb.

1049D	As 1049B civil freighter, but max gross weight 133,000lb. Four built for Seaboard; two modified up to 1049H/03 standard with 135,400lb gross weight.	1549	As 1449, but 10ft 9in fuselage stretch over the Super Connie. Max gross weight 187,500lb and landing weight 137,500lb.
1049E	As 1049C, but with all structural modifications (except to the undercarriage) for an eventual take-off weight of 150,000lb. Some later modified to 1049G standard.	1649A	As 1449 but with 'EA-2 Turbo-Compounds mounted 5ft further outboard and no fuselage stretch. Max gross weight 156,000lb and landing weight 123,000lb. Some later converted to freighters. Gross weight later increased to 160,000lb.
1049E/01	As 1049E, but max take-off weight 135,400lb; same landing weight.		
1049E/02	As 1049E, but max take-off weight 135,400lb and landing weight raised to 113,000lb.	1649	W2V-1 radar picket development of 1649A projected with 150ft span wing, 'saucer' radome as on WV-2E and Allison T-56 turboprops plus two Westinghouse J34 jets in wing-tip pods. Central fin and rudder deleted.
1049F	C-121C, the USAF version of the R7V-1, with max gross weight of 137,500lb. R-3350-91 Turbo-Compounds. 33 built.		
1049F	VC-121E *Columbine III* for President Eisenhower.	1049B	TC-121C. Convertible passenger/cargo version of RC-121C with radar and electronics removed. Max gross weight 124,300lb. Nine RC-121Cs converted to TC-121Cs; one further modified to JC-121C standard.
1049F	JC-121C. Two C-121Cs, 54-160 and 54-178 modified for special electronics tests with radomes fitted; later designated EC-121C. Also TC-121C 51-3841.		
1049F	Several C-121Cs and C-121Gs modified to EC-121S standard for Pennsylvania Air National Guard's Tactical Electronic Warfare Squadron.	1049A-55	EC-121D. Modified RC-121D with special electronics installation.
		1049A	NC-121D 56-6956 (ex-EC-121K 143226). Modified to take the Bendix TRAP III airborne radiation measurement system.
1049G	Development of 1049E with 'DA-3 Turbo-Compounds; tip tanks and weather radar optional 'extras'. Max gross weight 137,500lb and landing weight 113,000lb. Several later converted to freighters.	1049A	EC-121H. RC-121Ds and one EC-121K modified to carry extra ton of electronics to transmit to SAGE ground installations. Smaller dorsal radome ahead of the main one.
1049H	Freighter version of 1049G with the 1049D's freight doors and heavy-duty floor, convertible to seat up to 118 passengers. Max weight 137,500lb with 'EA-3 engines or 140,000lb with 'EA-6s.	1049B-55	TC-121G classified modification of C-121G.
		1049B-55	TC-121J classified modification of C-121J.
		1049A	JC-121K. Special test (temporary) modification—prefix 'J' in designation—of EC-121K 143196 for US Army in connection with missile tracking. No ventral radome. Also JEC-121K 141304.
1049H/03	Two Seaboard 1049Ds modified up to this standard with 'DA-3 engines, tip tanks and max gross weight of 135,400lb, later 137,500lb.		
1149	Proposed turboprop conversion of 1049 dated November 1951.	1049A	NC-121K. Four EC-121Ks and one EC-121M modified for special test (permanent) duties—prefix 'N' in designation. One used for Project Magnet programme, one for oceanographic surveys with dorsal and ventral radomes deleted. Also one NEC-121K.
1249	Two R7V-2 test beds for P & W T-34 turboprops with Turbo-Hydromatic broad chord airscrews. Cruising speed 440mph and max gross weight 150,000lb.		
1249	Two more R7V-2s transferred to USAF as YC-121Fs for T-34 testing; at first designated C-134-LO. Tip tanks fitted.	1049A	EC-121N. As WC-121N, with special electronics installation.
		1049A	EC-121P. Several EC-121Ks modified for Navy with additional electronics for anti-submarine duties.
1249	R7V-2 re-engined with four 3,750ehp Allison 501-D13 turboprops for Electra test programme.	1049A	RC-121Q. One specially modified RC-121D, details not available.
1249A	Proposed civil freighter version of R7V-2 with PT2F-1 (civil T-34) turboprops.	1049A	EC-121R. Several Navy EC-121Ps modified for USAF as electronic data relay aircraft for use in South East Asia.
1249B	Proposed passenger version of 1249A similar to 1049E; max gross weight 150,000lb.	1049F	EC-121S. See under C-121C.
1349	Designation not used.	1049A	EC-121T. New variant of EC-121D, details classified.
1449	Maximum range Super Connie project with new thinner wing of 150ft span, PT2F-1 turboprops and 4ft 7in fuselage stretch. Max gross weight 177,000lb. Redesigned and strengthened undercarriage.	1049	Test bed for SNECMA-Turboméca M49 Larzac turbofan jet. First flew 2 March 1971 with new engine.

Bibliography

In addition to notes kept by the author over a period of some years and Lockheed and airline press releases and cuttings, the following books and periodicals have been drawn upon for information on the Lockheed Constellation:

Anderson, Holmes G. *The Lockheed Constellation*—Profile No 120, Profile Publications Ltd, Windsor, Berkshire.

Davies, R. E. G. *A History of the World's Airlines*, 1964.

Gill, Frederick W. and Bates, Gilbert L. *Airline Competition*, Division of Research, Harvard Business School, Boston 63, Mass, USA, 1948.

Hibbard, Hall and Johnson, C. L. 'The First Constellation Decade', paper presented at the SAE Golden Anniversary Meeting in New York; *Shell Aviation News* No 211, January 1956.

Constellation, The, edited by Peter Marson, Air-Britain Monograph, published by Air-Britain, Brentwood, Essex, 1969.

Jane's All The World's Aircraft.

Johnson, C. L. *Development of the Lockheed Constellation*, published by Lockheed, Burbank, California.

Lockheed Story, The, November 1955, published by Lockheed.

'Plane That Grew, The,' *Aero Digest*, June 1951.

World Airline Record, 1965 edition, Roadcap & Associates, Chicago, USA.

ABC World Airways Guide

The Aeroplane

Air Pictorial

American Aviation, also known as *Airlift*

Esso Air World

Flight

Overseas Airline News and other Air-Britain publications

Shell Aviation News

Acknowledgements

The author is particularly indebted to Philip L. Juergens of Lockheed, P. J. Marson, Peter Keating, J. M. G. Gradidge, John P. Stewart and Ann Tilbury of *Flight International* for their assistance in providing photographs for this book. Grateful acknowledgement is also made to the following:

Air France, p. 114; BOAC, p. 39 (bottom); T. Breese, p. 75; R. Caratini, pp. 28, 35, 37; Compagnie Générale des Turbo-Machines, p. 73 (both); El Al Israel Airlines, p. 26; *Esso Air World*, p. 99 (bottom); Federal Aviation Administration, pp. 44, 120; Jim Flannery's, p. 96 (bottom); *Flight International*, pp. 18, 21, 23, 24, 25, 39 (top), 40 (top), 41 (top), p. 45, 60 (bottom), 61 (both), 111; C. Jansson, pp. 29 (l. & r.), 30 (top), 98 (bottom), 117; Peter R. Keating, pp. 91 (both), 100, 106; KLM, pp. 34, 65; Lockheed Aircraft, pp. 9, 10, 11, 13, 14, 15, 16, 19, 20, 22, 43, 54, 56 (both), 57, 58 (both), 59 (top), 60 (top), 62, 65, 67, 70, 71, 72, 77, 79 (bottom), 88 (top); Lockheed Aircraft Service Co., pp. 51, 83 (bottom), 84, 89; Lufthansa, pp. 93 (top), 115; P. J. Marson, pp. 59 (bottom), 93 (bottom); Military Aircraft Storage and Disposition Centre, p. 80; R. O'Dell, p. 96 (top); D. Olson, pp. 27, 30 (bottom), 40 (bottom), 41 (bottom), 48, 50 (l), 74, 95, 97, 99 (top), 102, 118; D. Ostrowski, p. 31; Qantas, p. 90; Reuter via *Flight*, p. 46; E. M. Sommerich, p. 101; John P. Stewart, pp. 50 (r), 78 (both), 82, 83 (top), 85, 98 (top); via J. W. R. Taylor, p. 33; N. E. Taylor, p. 76 (top); Trans World Airlines, pp. 88 (bottom), 107; USAAF Air Transport Command, p. 17; Varig, p. 92; J. T. Wible, p. 81 (bottom).

Index

DATE DUE

AUG 15 1974		
NOV 2 9 1978		
JAN 15 1979		
APR 08 1979		
NOV 1 1981 1982		
AUG 3 1982		
JUL 08 1983		
FEB 5 1984		
MAR 5 '85		
AUG 8 '86		
OCT 28 '87		
FEB 12 '88		
NOV 2 3 1991		
NOV 1 8 1991		
MAR 1 1 1992		
APR 2 0 1992		
		PRINTED IN U.S.A.
GAYLORD		